Editor

Erica N. Russikoff, M.A.

Illustrator

Clint McKnight

Cover Artist

Brenda DiAntonis

Editor in Chief

Ina Massler Levin, M.A.

Creative Director

Karen J. Goldfluss, M.S. Ed.

Art Coordinator

Renée Christine Yates

Imaging

Craig Gunnell

Publisher

Mary D. Smith, M.S. Ed.

Differentiated Nonfiction Reading

GRADE 2

Includes Standards & Benchmarks

- Each passage is written at 3 different levels: easier, average, more challenging
- Content areas include Science, Geography, History, and Language Arts

Author

Tracie I. Heskett, M. Ed.

Teacher Created Resources, Inc.
6421 Industry Way
Westminster, CA 92683
www.teachercreated.com

ISBN: 978-1-4206-2919-4

© 2010 Teacher Created Resources, Inc.
Made in U.S.A.

Teacher Created Resources

Table of Contents

Introduction

If you are like most teachers, your classroom includes a wide variety of students: average students, English language learners, gifted students, and learning disabled students. You may be expected to get your diverse student population, including special education students and those for whom English is a second language, to master grade-level, content-area material. That's a challenging task and one that requires grade-level, content-area materials written at several levels. *Differentiated Nonfiction Reading* was written specifically to help you respond to the demands of your state and local standards while meeting the needs of your students.

Purpose of This Book

Each passage in *Differentiated Nonfiction Reading* covers a grade-level appropriate curriculum topic in science, geography, history, or language arts. The Mid-continent Research for Education and Learning (McREL) standard and benchmark related to each passage is listed on pages 9–12.

Each content-area passage is written at three different levels: easy (below grade level), average (at grade level), and challenging (above grade level). After each passage is a set of comprehension questions that all of your students will answer. This enables your students to access the text and concepts at their instructional—rather than frustration—level, while requiring them to meet objective standards, just as they must do on standardized assessments.

Prepare Your Students to Read Content-Area Text

You can prepare your students to read the passages in *Differentiated Nonfiction Reading* by daily reading aloud a short nonfiction selection from another source. Reading content-area text aloud is critical to developing your students' ability to read it themselves.

Discussing content-area concepts with your class is also very important. Remember, however, that discussion can never replace reading aloud since people do not speak using the vocabulary and complex sentence structures of written language.

Readability

All of the passages in *Differentiated Nonfiction Reading* have a reading level that has been calculated by the Flesch-Kincaid Readability Formula. This formula, built into Microsoft Word®, determines a text's readability by calculating the number of words, syllables, and sentences.

Each passage is presented at three levels: easy, average, and challenging. *Easy* is below second-grade level; *average* is at second-grade level; and *challenging* is above second-grade level. The chart on page 13 shows you the specific reading levels of every passage.

To ensure that only you know the reading level at which each student is working, the levels are not printed on the passages. Instead, at the top of the page is a set of books with a specific pattern that will allow you to quickly match students and passages.

Pattern			
Reading Level	**easy** (below grade level)	**average** (at grade level)	**challenging** (above grade level)

Introduction (cont.)

Essential Comprehension Skills

Comprehension is the primary goal of any reading task. Students who comprehend expository text not only do better on tests, but they also have more opportunities in life. *Differentiated Nonfiction Reading* will help you to promote the foundation of comprehension skills necessary for a lifetime of learning. The questions following each passage always appear in the same order and cover six vital comprehension skills:

1. **Locating facts**—Questions based on exactly what the text states—*who, what, when, where, why,* and *how many*

2. **Understanding vocabulary in context**—Questions based on the ability to infer word meaning from the syntax and semantics of the surrounding text, as well as the ability to recognize known synonyms and antonyms for a newly encountered word

3. **Determining sequence**—Questions based on chronological order—what happened *first, last,* and *in between*

4. **Identifying conditions**—Questions that ask students to identify similarities and differences or notice cause-and-effect relationships

5. **Making inferences**—Questions that require students to evaluate, to make decisions, and to draw logical conclusions

6. **Analyzing and visualizing**—Questions that make students draw upon their schema and/or visualization skills to select the correct response (Visualization reinforces the important skill of picturing the text.)

How to Use This Book

You can choose to do whole-class or independent practice. For whole-group practice, you can:

1. Distribute the passages based on students' instructional reading levels.

2. Have students read the text silently and answer the questions either on the comprehension questions page or on one of the Answer Sheets on pages 94–95.

3. Collect all of the papers and score them.

4. Return the comprehension questions pages or Answer Sheets to the students, and discuss how they determined their answers.

5. Point out how students had to use their background knowledge to answer certain questions.

You may distribute the passages without revealing the different levels. There are several ways to approach this. If you do not want your students to be aware that the passages are differentiated, organize the passages in small piles by seating arrangement. Then, when you approach a group of desks, you have just the levels you need. An alternative is to make a pile of passages from diamonds to polka dots. Put a finger between the top two levels. Then, as you approach each student, pull the passage from the top (easy), middle (average), or bottom (challenging) layer. You will need to do this quickly and without much hesitation.

You can also announce to your class that all students will read at their own instructional levels. Do not discuss the technicalities of how the reading levels were determined. Just state that every person is reading at his or her own level and then answering the same questions. By making this statement, you can make distributing the three different levels a straightforward process.

Introduction *(cont.)*

How to Use This Book *(cont.)*

If you find that a student is doing well, try giving him or her the next-level-up passage the next time. If he or she displays frustration, be ready to slip the student the lower-level passage.

If you prefer to have the students work independently or in centers, follow this procedure:

1. Create a folder for each student.

2. If needed, make photocopies of the Answer Sheet on page 95 for each class member, and staple the Answer Sheet to the back of each student folder.

3. Each time you want to use a passage, place the appropriate reading level of the passage and the associated comprehension questions in each student's folder.

4. Have students retrieve their folders, read the passage, and answer the questions.

5. Go over the answers with the whole class, or check the folders individually at a convenient time.

6. As an option, you may want to provide a laminated copy of the Answer Key on page 96 in the center, so students can check their own papers.

Teaching Multiple-Choice Response

Whichever method you choose for using this book, it's a good idea to practice as a class how to read a passage and respond to the comprehension questions. In this way, you can demonstrate your own thought processes by "thinking aloud" to figure out an answer. Essentially, this means that you tell your students your thoughts as they come to you.

First, make copies of the practice comprehension questions on page 8, and distribute them to your class. Then, make and display an overhead transparency of the practice reading passage on page 7. Next, read the passage chorally. Studies have found that students of all ages enjoy choral reading, and it is especially helpful for English language learners. Choral reading lets students practice reading fluently in a safe venue because they can read in a whisper or even drop out if they feel the need.

Discuss Question 1: After you've read the passage aloud, ask a student to read the first question aloud. Tell the student NOT to answer the question. Instead, read all of the answer choices aloud. Emphasize that reading the choices first is always the best way to approach any multiple-choice question. Since this question is about *locating facts*, reread the fourth paragraph of the passage aloud as the class follows along. Have the students reread the question silently and make a selection based on the information found. Ask a student who gives the correct response (C) to explain his or her reasoning. Explain that the first question is always the easiest because the fact is stated right in the passage.

Discuss Question 2: The second question is about the *vocabulary* word shown in boldfaced print in the passage. Ask a student to read the question aloud. Teach your students to reread the sentence before, the sentence with, and the sentence after the vocabulary word in the passage. This will give them a context and help them to figure out what the word means. Then, have them substitute the word choices given for the vocabulary term in the passage. For each choice, they should reread the sentence with the substituted word and ask themselves, "Does this make sense?" This will help them to identify the best choice. One by one, substitute the words into the sentence, and read the sentence aloud. It will be obvious which one makes the most sense (B).

Teaching Multiple-Choice Response *(cont.)*

Discuss Question 3: The third question asks about *sequence*. Ask a student to read the question aloud. Write the choices on chart paper or the board. As a class, determine their order of occurrence, and write the numbers one through four next to them. Then, reread the question and make the correct choice (A).

Discuss Question 4: The fourth question is about *cause and effect* or *similarities and differences*. Ask a student to read the question aloud. Teach your students to look for the key word(s) in the question ("penguins") and search for the specific word(s) in the passage. Explain that they may need to think about what they already know about the key word to determine how it is alike or different from something else. For this question, ask your students to show where they found the correct response in the passage. Have students explain in their own words how they figured out the correct answer (B). This may be time-consuming at first, but it is an excellent way to help your students learn from each other.

Discuss Question 5: The fifth question asks students to make an *inference*. Ask a student to read the question aloud. Tell your students your thoughts as they occur to you, such as: "Well, the article didn't say that you need to have a camera, so that one's questionable. The article did say that you should not bring animals. So I'll get rid of that choice. You could get there by boat. But it would be a very long trip. I don't think that's the best choice here. Let's look back at the passage . . . it states that all visitors must go with a guide. The word "must" means you have to have it, so I'm going to select D."

Discuss Question 6: The sixth question calls for *analysis* or *visualization*. With such questions, some of the answers may be stated in the passage, but others may have different wording. Sometimes one or more of the answers must be visualized to ascertain the correct response.

After having a student read the question aloud, you can say, "This one is tricky. It's asking me to choose the one that *will not* instead of the one that *will*. First, let's look at all the choices. Then, we can ask ourselves which ones are not mentioned in the article. Only one of these animals is not listed in the article." Then, read the answer choices aloud and eliminate them one by one. Point out that the passage does not state that there are any tigers on the islands, which is how you identify the correct answer (D).

Frequent Practice Is Ideal

The passages and comprehension questions in *Differentiated Nonfiction Reading* are time-efficient, allowing your students to practice these skills often. The more your students practice reading and responding to content-area comprehension questions, the more confident and competent they will become. Set aside time to allow your class to do every passage. If you do so, you'll be pleased with your students' improved comprehension of any nonfiction text, both within your classroom and beyond its walls.

Extreme Wildlife Adventure

If you like wildlife, you will enjoy the Galapagos Islands. You can dive in the ocean or stay on land. The islands are far away from the mainland. They are 600 miles off the coast.

Volcanoes in the ocean erupted. They formed islands. Each island is a volcano. Some are still active.

The islands are slowly moving eastward. Hot rock on the ocean floor makes land move. The islands drift in the ocean.

There are large islands. Some are tiny. There are more than twenty islands total. People live on just five of the islands.

Amazing animals live there. There are penguins. No other penguins live in the tropics. There are iguanas that swim. They eat seaweed.

The animals do not fear humans. The islands have no large predators. People can walk right by the animals. Blue-footed booby birds dance by your feet. Sea lions swim near by. You can see an **albatross** fly above you. A giant tortoise might walk by.

People can go diving. A boat leaves from the main island. The trip takes fifteen hours. It goes to other islands.

There are strong ocean currents. Dive to a ledge sixty feet down. Grab onto the rock and hang on. Watch the marine life swim by.

A diver can see whale sharks. There are manta rays and dolphins. Sea turtles swim by.

People try to preserve the islands. They do not want them to change. Do not bring animals from other places. They eat the same food as native animals. It is hard for native animals to survive.

Almost all of the land area is a national park. All visitors must go with a guide. It is fun to explore and learn about the wildlife.

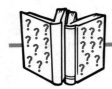

Extreme Wildlife Adventure

Directions: Darken the best answer choice.

1. On how many islands do people live?
   - Ⓐ 600
   - Ⓑ 20
   - Ⓒ 5
   - Ⓓ 15

2. An **albatross** is
   - Ⓐ a boat that travels on the ocean.
   - Ⓑ a large seabird with long wings.
   - Ⓒ a bird that dances by your feet.
   - Ⓓ a tree with coconuts.

3. When you dive in strong ocean currents, what should you do first?
   - Ⓐ Dive to a ledge.
   - Ⓑ Hang onto the rock.
   - Ⓒ Grab onto the rock.
   - Ⓓ Watch sea animals.

4. How are penguins in the Galapagos different from other penguins?
   - Ⓐ They do not look like penguins.
   - Ⓑ They do not live at the South Pole.
   - Ⓒ They do not swim.
   - Ⓓ They do not eat fish.

5. What do you need to have to visit the Galapagos?
   - Ⓐ a camera
   - Ⓑ a boat
   - Ⓒ an animal
   - Ⓓ a guide

6. Picture a tour on the Galapagos islands. What will you *not* see?
   - Ⓐ a booby bird with blue feet
   - Ⓑ a sea lion
   - Ⓒ a giant tortoise
   - Ⓓ a tiger

Standards Correlation

Each passage and comprehension question in *Differentiated Nonfiction Reading* meets at least one of the following standards and benchmarks, which are used with permission from McREL. Copyright 2010 McREL. Mid-continent Research for Education and Learning, 4601 DTC Boulevard, Suite 500, Denver, CO 80237. Telephone: 303-337-0990. Web site: *www.mcrel.org/standards-benchmarks*

Standards and Benchmarks	Passage Title	Pages
SCIENCE		
Standard 5. Understands the structure and function of cells and organisms **Benchmark 1.** Knows the basic needs of plants and animals (e.g., air, water, nutrients, light or food, shelter) **Benchmark 2.** Knows that plants and animals have features that help them live in different environments	A New Monkey Komodo Dragons	14–17 26–29
Standard 6. Understands relationships among organisms and their physical environment **Benchmark 1.** Knows that plants and animals need certain resources for energy and growth (e.g., food, water, light, air) **Benchmark 2.** Knows that living things are found almost everywhere in the world and that distinct environments support the life of different types of plants and animals	A New Monkey Komodo Dragons	14–17 26–29
Standard 9. Understands the sources and properties of energy **Benchmark 1.** Knows that the sun supplies heat and light to Earth **Benchmark 4.** Knows that sound is produced by vibrating objects	Wind Power The Sounds We Hear	22–25 30–33
Standard 10. Understands forces and motion **Benchmark 1.** Knows that magnets can be used to make some things move without being touched	Wind Power	22–25
Standard 12. Understands the nature of scientific inquiry **Benchmark 1.** Knows that learning can come from careful observations and simple experiments **Benchmark 2.** Knows that tools (e.g., thermometers, magnifiers, rulers, balances) can be used to gather information and extend the senses	Meet Astronaut Danny Olivas	18–21
GEOGRAPHY		
Standard 1. Understands the characteristics and uses of maps, globes, and other geographic tools and technologies **Benchmark 1.** Understands the globe as a representation of Earth	Find Your Way	34–37

Standards Correlation (cont.)

Standards and Benchmarks	Passage Title	Pages
GEOGRAPHY (cont.)		
Standard 3. Understands the characteristics and uses of spatial organization of Earth's surface **Benchmark 1.** Identifies physical and human features in terms of the four spatial elements (e.g., locations [point], transportation and communication routes [line], regions [area], lakes filled with water [volume])	The Shape of the Land	50–53
Standard 4. Understands the physical and human characteristics of place **Benchmark 1.** Knows the physical and human characteristics of the local community (e.g., neighborhoods, schools, parks, creeks, shopping areas, airports, museums, sports stadiums, hospitals)	Let's Play	38–41
Standard 5. Understands the concepts of regions **Benchmark 1.** Knows areas that can be classified as regions according to physical criteria (e.g., landform regions, soil regions, vegetation regions, climate regions, water basins) and human criteria (e.g., political regions, population regions, economic regions, language regions)	Deserts The Shape of the Land	42–45 50–53
Standard 7. Knows the physical processes that shape patterns on Earth's surface	The Shape of the Land	50–53
Standard 15. Understands how physical systems affect human systems	The Biggest Waves	46–49
ECONOMICS		
Standard 1. Understands that scarcity of productive resources requires choices that generate opportunity costs **Benchmark 1.** Knows that goods are objects that can satisfy people's wants, and services are activities that can satisfy people's wants **Benchmark 2.** Understands that since people cannot have everything they want, they must make choices about using goods and services to satisfy wants **Benchmark 3.** Knows that a cost is what you give up when you decide to do something, and a benefit is something that satisfies your wants **Benchmark 8.** Knows that choices about what goods and services to buy and consume determine how resources will be used	To Buy or Not to Buy (Web Page)	86–89
Standard 3. Understands the concept of prices and the interaction of supply and demand in a market economy **Benchmark 1.** Knows that a price is the amount of money that people pay when they buy a good or service	To Buy or Not to Buy (Web Page)	86–89

Standards Correlation *(cont.)*

Standards and Benchmarks	Passage Title	Pages
ECONOMICS *(cont.)*		
Standard 4. Understands basic features of market structures **Benchmark 1.** Understands that in an exchange people trade goods and services for other goods and services or for money **Benchmark 2.** Knows that money is a good that can be used to buy all other goods and services **Benchmark 3.** Understands that when two people trade because they want to, they expect to be better off after the exchange **Benchmark 4.** Knows that barter is trading goods and services for other goods and services without using money	Money	54–57
Standard 6. Understands the roles government plays in the United States economy **Benchmark 1.** Knows that some of the goods and services we use are provided by the government	Money	54–57
HISTORY		
Standard 1. Understands family life now and in the past, and family life in various places long ago **Benchmark 3.** Knows the cultural similarities and differences in clothes, homes, food, communication, technology, and cultural traditions between families now and in the past	Dogs as Pets	70–73
Standard 2. Understands the history of a local community and how communities in North America varied long ago **Benchmark 5.** Understands life in a pioneer farming community (e.g., the Old Northwest, the prairies, the Southwest, eastern Canada, the Far West)	An Apple a Day	62–65
Standard 4. Understands how democratic values came to be, and how they have been exemplified by people, events, and symbols **Benchmark 2.** Understands how individuals have worked to achieve the liberties and equality promised in the principles of American democracy and to improve the lives of people from many groups (e.g., Rosa Parks, Martin Luther King Jr., Sojourner Truth, Cesar Chavez) **Benchmark 5.** Understands how important figures reacted to their times and why they were significant to the history of our democracy (e.g., George Washington, Thomas Jefferson, Abraham Lincoln, Sojourner Truth, Susan B. Anthony, Mary McLeod Bethune, Eleanor Roosevelt, Martin Luther King Jr.)	Fight for Freedom	58–61

Standards Correlation *(cont.)*

Standards and Benchmarks	Passage Title	Pages
HISTORY *(cont.)*		
Standard 4. *(cont.)* **Benchmark 6.** Understands the ways in which people in a variety of fields have advanced the cause of human rights, equality, and the common good (e.g., Frederick Douglass, Clara Barton, Elizabeth Blackwell, Jackie Robinson, Rosa Parks, Jonas Salk, Cesar Chavez)	Fight for Freedom	58–61
Standard 6. Understands the folklore and other cultural contributions from various regions of the United States and how they helped to form a national heritage **Benchmark 1.** Knows regional folk heroes, stories, or songs that have contributed to the development of the cultural history of the U.S. (e.g., Pecos Bill, Brer Rabbit, Paul Bunyan, Davy Crockett, John Henry, Joe Magarac) **Benchmark 2.** Knows the differences between toys and games children played long ago and the toys and games of today	An Apple a Day Score the Goal!	62–65 66–69
LANGUAGE ARTS*		
Standard 5. Uses the general skills and strategies of the reading process **Benchmark 4.** Uses basic elements of structural analysis to decode unknown words (e.g., syllables, basic prefixes and suffixes, root words, common spelling patterns, contractions) **Benchmark 6.** Understands level-appropriate sight words and vocabulary (e.g., words for persons, places, things; frequency words such as *said*, *was*, and *where*)	The Storyteller (Back of Book) The World of Cartoons (Encyclopedia Entry) Learn to Draw (How-to Page) To Buy or Not to Buy (Web Page) The Many Uses of Pumpkins (Magazine Article)	74–77 78–81 82–85 86–89 90–93
Standard 7. Uses reading skills and strategies to understand and interpret a variety of informational texts **Benchmark 1.** Uses reading skills and strategies to understand a variety of informational texts (e.g., written directions, signs, captions, warning labels, informational books, biographical sketches) **Benchmark 4.** Relates new information to prior knowledge and experience	The Storyteller (Back of Book) The World of Cartoons (Encyclopedia Entry) Learn to Draw (How-to Page) To Buy or Not to Buy (Web Page) The Many Uses of Pumpkins (Magazine Article)	74–77 78–81 82–85 86–89 90–93

*Every passage in this book meets the language arts standard of some or all of these benchmarks. The language arts passages are listed here because they were designed to specifically address these benchmarks.

Reading Levels Chart

Content Area and Title	Easy ◇	Average ★	Challenging ○
SCIENCE			
A New Monkey	1.9	2.6	3.6
Meet Astronaut Danny Olivas	1.6	2.3	3.1
Wind Power	1.9	2.6	3.5
Komodo Dragons	1.9	2.9	3.9
The Sounds We Hear	1.6	2.9	3.5
GEOGRAPHY			
Find Your Way	1.2	2.4	3.3
Let's Play	1.8	2.5	3.1
Deserts	1.8	2.4	3.3
The Biggest Waves	1.9	2.9	3.8
The Shape of the Land	1.8	2.8	3.5
HISTORY			
Money	1.8	2.5	3.4
Fight for Freedom	1.4	2.5	3.3
An Apple a Day	1.9	2.1	3.0
Score the Goal!	1.5	2.2	3.1
Dogs as Pets	1.9	2.1	3.7
LANGUAGE ARTS			
The Storyteller (Back of Book)	1.8	2.6	3.7
The World of Cartoons (Encyclopedia Entry)	1.8	2.1	3.2
Learn to Draw (How-to Page)	1.6	2.1	3.1
To Buy or Not to Buy (Web Page)	1.7	2.8	3.6
The Many Uses of Pumpkins (Magazine Article)	1.7	2.4	3.2

A New Monkey

There is a new group of monkeys. They are called Kipunji. These monkeys live in Africa. They live in the mountains. They live only in this **remote** area.

These monkeys are rare. Less than 1,000 of the monkeys live in the wild. They are in danger.

Many things can hurt the monkeys. People hunt them for meat. People also hunt them because the monkeys eat farm crops. The monkeys live in forests. People log the forests. This destroys the forests.

These monkeys have long hair. It keeps them warm. It gets cold in the winter. They have brown to off-white hair. The end of the tail is off-white. They have black hands and feet.

The monkeys live in trees. Sometimes they come down from the trees. They come down to eat. Sometimes they fight with other monkeys.

Kipunji live in groups. The monkeys like fruit. They eat flowers. They eat leaves and bark. They also eat moss. They are active during the day.

Natives say the monkeys are shy. People destroy their habitat.

Hunters live in towns. They live by a mountain. They told scientists about the monkeys.

Scientists first saw the monkeys in 2003. They watched them again later. Scientists want the monkeys to live. They want to learn about this new kind of monkey.

A New Monkey

There is a new group of monkeys. They are called Kipunji. These monkeys live in Africa. They live in the mountains of Tanzania. This **remote** area is the only place they live.

These monkeys are rare. Less than 1,000 of the monkeys live in the wild. They are endangered.

Many things threaten the monkeys. People hunt them for meat. People also hunt them because the monkeys eat farm crops. People log the forests where they live. Logging destroys the forests.

These monkeys have long hair. It keeps them warm in the cold winter. Their hair is brown to off-white. The tail is off-white on the end. They have black hands and feet.

The monkeys live in trees. Sometimes they come down from the trees. They come down to eat. They leave the trees if they fight with other monkeys.

They live in groups. The monkeys like fruit. They eat flowers, leaves, and bark. They also eat lichen and moss. They are active during the day.

Natives say the monkeys are shy. People keep destroying their habitat.

Hunters live in villages. They live by a mountain. They told scientists about the monkeys.

Scientists first saw them in May 2003. They watched them again in December 2003. Scientists want these monkeys to survive. They want to learn about the new species of monkey.

A New Monkey

There is a new group of monkeys. They are called Kipunji. These monkeys live in Africa. They live in the mountains. This **remote** area is the only place they live.

These monkeys are rare. Scientists think that less than 1,000 of the monkeys live in the wild. They are critically endangered.

Many things threaten the monkeys. People hunt them for meat. People also hunt them because the monkeys eat farm crops. People log in the forests where they live. The forests are being destroyed.

These monkeys have long hair. It keeps them warm in the cold winter. Their hair is brown to off-white. The tail is off-white on the end. They have black hands and feet.

The monkeys live in trees. Sometimes they come down to eat. They also leave the trees if they have a conflict with another group of monkeys.

They live in groups. The monkeys eat fruit, flowers, leaves, bark, lichen, and moss. They are active during the day.

Natives describe Kipunji as shy monkeys. Their habitat keeps being destroyed.

Hunters in villages around Mt. Rungwe told scientists about the monkeys.

Scientists first saw them in May 2003. They observed them more closely in December 2003. Scientists want these monkeys to survive. They want to learn more about the new species of monkey.

A New Monkey

Directions: Darken the best answer choice.

1. How many Kipunji monkeys live in the wild?
   - Ⓐ less than 2
   - Ⓑ up to 35
   - Ⓒ about 40
   - Ⓓ less than 1,000

2. If a place is **remote**, it
   - Ⓐ turns on the TV.
   - Ⓑ is isolated.
   - Ⓒ gets really hot.
   - Ⓓ is by the ocean.

3. What happened first?
   - Ⓐ Scientists saw the monkeys.
   - Ⓑ Scientists watched the monkeys closely.
   - Ⓒ Hunters told scientists about shy monkeys.
   - Ⓓ Scientists learned more about the monkeys.

4. The monkeys have long hair, so
   - Ⓐ they can hide.
   - Ⓑ they can keep warm.
   - Ⓒ they can live in the trees.
   - Ⓓ they can eat moss.

5. Why do people hunt these monkeys?
   - Ⓐ The monkeys eat what farmers grow.
   - Ⓑ The monkeys like fruit.
   - Ⓒ The monkeys live in the forest.
   - Ⓓ The monkeys have long tails.

6. Picture Kipunji monkeys in the forest. What do you see?
   - Ⓐ a monkey by itself
   - Ⓑ a monkey eating flowers
   - Ⓒ a monkey living on the ground
   - Ⓓ a monkey with white hands and feet

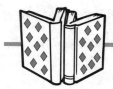

Meet Astronaut Danny Olivas

We wonder what it is like in outer space. People travel in space. We call them **astronauts**. They tell us what they find. Danny Olivas traveled in space.

Danny was born in California. He grew up in Texas. He wanted to make things. He went to college. He won awards.

Danny set goals. He worked hard. He wanted to go into space. He is an example. Anyone can go into space.

Danny worked at an air force base. He made spacesuits better. He worked on rockets. Danny made things to use in space.

Danny had a lot to learn. He trained to go into space. He read a lot. He prepared for danger in bad weather. He learned how to survive.

Astronauts practice in a machine. They pretend it is a rocket. It feels like being in space.

Danny's teacher inspired him. He asked her to come to the shuttle launch. It was a great day. His teacher, Ms. Martha Pickrell, was there.

Danny was ready. He flew on a space shuttle. He helped with the mission. He went to the Space Station. Danny walked in space.

NASA gave him a new job. Danny helped crews in orbit. They talked to the ground crew. They told NASA if something went wrong.

Danny likes to walk in space. He wants to learn more about space.

Meet Astronaut Danny Olivas

We wonder what it is like in outer space. People travel in space. We call them **astronauts**. They tell us what they find. Danny Olivas knows what it is like to go into space.

Danny was born in California. He grew up in Texas. He wanted to make things. He went to college. His work won awards.

Danny set goals. He worked hard to go into space. He is an example. People from all backgrounds can go into space.

Danny worked at an air force base. He made spacesuits better. He worked on rocket engines. Danny worked on things to use in space.

Danny had a lot to learn. It takes training to go into outer space. He read a lot. He prepared for danger in bad weather. He learned how to survive.

Astronauts practice in a special machine. They pretend they are in a rocket. It is like being in space.

Many people help us reach our goals. Danny's sixth-grade teacher, Martha Pickrell, inspired him. He asked her to come to the space shuttle launch. Ms. Pickrell was there for a great day in his life.

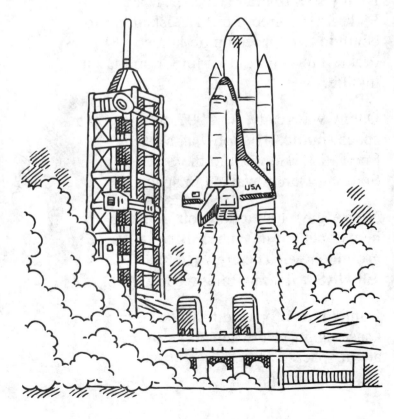

Danny was ready. In 2007, he flew on a space shuttle. His job was Mission Expert. He went to the Space Station. Danny walked in space.

NASA gave him a new job in 2008. Danny helped crews in orbit. They talked to the ground crew. They could tell NASA if something went wrong.

Danny looks forward to walking in space again. He wants to learn more about space.

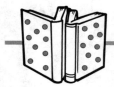

Meet Astronaut Danny Olivas

We wonder what it is like in outer space. **Astronauts** travel in space. They tell us what they find. Danny Olivas knows what it is like to go into space.

Danny was born in California. He grew up in Texas. He wanted to be an engineer. He went to college. His work won awards.

Danny set goals. He worked hard to go into space. He is an example. People from all backgrounds can go into space.

Danny worked at an air force base. He made spacesuits better. He worked on rocket engines. Danny worked on things to use in space.

Danny trained to go into outer space. He read a lot. He prepared for emergencies in bad weather. He learned how to survive.

Astronauts practice in a special machine called a simulator. They pretend they are in a rocket. It is like being in space.

Danny's sixth grade teacher, Martha Pickrell, inspired him. He asked her to come to the space shuttle launch. Ms. Pickrell took part in an important day in his life.

Danny was ready. In 2007, he flew on a space shuttle. His job was Mission Specialist. He went to the Space Station. Danny walked in space.

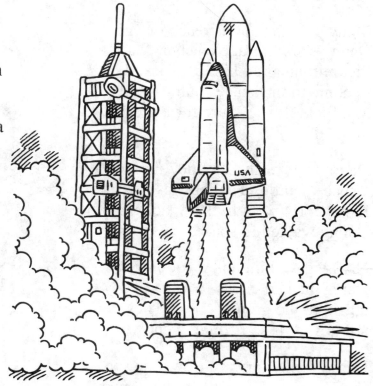

NASA gave him a new job in 2008. He helped people in space talk to the ground crew. The crews in orbit could tell NASA if something went wrong.

Danny looks forward to walking in space again. He wants to learn more about space.

Meet Astronaut Danny Olivas

Directions: Darken the best answer choice.

1. Who came to watch the space shuttle launch?
   Ⓐ a robot
   Ⓑ Danny's teacher
   Ⓒ crews in orbit
   Ⓓ Danny's mother

2. An **astronaut** is someone who
   Ⓐ makes things.
   Ⓑ reads books.
   Ⓒ travels in space.
   Ⓓ walks on the ground.

3. Before Danny went into space, he
   Ⓐ pretended he was in a rocket.
   Ⓑ walked in space.
   Ⓒ went to the Space Station.
   Ⓓ helped crews in orbit.

4. To go into outer space, astronauts have to
   Ⓐ win an award.
   Ⓑ teach.
   Ⓒ train.
   Ⓓ talk to the crew.

5. Where is the Space Station?
   Ⓐ Texas
   Ⓑ the space launch
   Ⓒ NASA
   Ⓓ outer space

6. Picture the space shuttle launch. What do you see?
   Ⓐ a rocket
   Ⓑ a train
   Ⓒ a telephone
   Ⓓ a school

Wind Power

All energy comes from the sun. We use energy to make things move. It gives us power.

The sun does not heat Earth evenly. High pressure moves to be equal with low pressure. Then, the wind blows.

Windmills use wind power. They have blades. The blades spin in the wind. They turn a turbine. It powers a **generator**.

The generator has a magnet. It spins on a pole. The magnet has coils of wire around it. The magnet spins. It makes electricity.

Wind turbines have a tail vane. It keeps the blades in the face of the wind. The wind needs to blow eleven to thirteen miles per hour for the blades to turn.

Some days have more wind than others. More electricity is made on these days. People use this extra power to move water from a low lake. The water moves to a higher lake. Sometimes the wind does not blow. People let the water out of the high lake. It flows down a tunnel. The water turns the turbines. It creates power.

People use wind for many things. Wind sails boats. Windmills grind grain. They pump water from the ground. Farmers use the water for their crops. A windmill can power a saw. People use the saw to cut wood.

Long ago, windmills crushed ore. They churned butter. They pumped water for indoor plumbing.

Some people think wind farms take up space. Farmers can grow crops on the land below wind turbines. Other people say wind farms make too much noise. They think wind farms block the view. Wind farms out in the ocean do not get in the way.

Wind power is safe and clean. It does not cause pollution. It takes no fuel to run a wind turbine. California has wind farms. They provide one-third of the world's wind power. People are thinking about using more wind power.

Wind Power

All energy comes from the sun. We use energy to make things move. Energy provides electricity.

The sun heats Earth unevenly. High pressure moves to be equal with low pressure. This creates wind.

Windmills use wind power. They have blades that spin in the wind. They turn a turbine. It powers a **generator**.

The generator has a magnet. It spins on a pole. The magnet has coils of wire around it. When the magnet spins, it makes electricity.

Wind turbines have a tail vane. It keeps the blades in the face of the wind. The wind needs to blow eleven to thirteen miles per hour for the blades to turn.

Some days have more wind than others. More electricity is made on these days. People use this extra power to move water from a low lake up to a higher lake. Sometimes the wind does not blow. People let the water out of the high lake. It flows down a tunnel. The water turns the turbines. It makes electricity when the wind does blow.

People use wind for many things. Wind sails boats. Windmills grind grain. They pump water from the ground. Farmers use the water for their crops. A windmill can power a saw. People use the saw to cut wood for building.

People in early America used windmills to crush ore. Windmills churned butter. They pumped water for indoor plumbing.

Some people think wind farms take up a lot of space. Farmers can grow crops on the land below wind turbines. Other people say wind farms make too much noise. They think wind farms block the view. Wind farms out in the ocean do not get in the way.

Wind power is safe and clean. It does not cause pollution. It takes no fuel to run a wind turbine. California has wind farms. They provide one-third of the world's wind power. People are thinking about using more wind power.

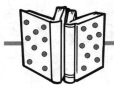

Wind Power

All energy comes from the sun. We use energy to make things move. Energy provides electricity.

The sun heats Earth unevenly. This causes uneven air pressure. High pressure moves to equalize with low pressure. This creates wind.

Windmills use wind power. They have blades that spin in the wind. They turn a turbine that powers a **generator**.

The generator has a magnet that spins on a pole. The magnet has coils of wire around it. When the magnet spins, it makes electricity.

Wind turbines have a tail vane. It keeps the blades in the face of the wind. The wind needs to blow eleven to thirteen miles per hour in order for the blades to turn.

Some days have more wind than others do. The wind turbines generate extra energy. The excess electricity pumps water from a low lake up to a higher lake. Sometimes the wind does not blow. People release the water from the high lake. It flows down a tunnel. The water turns the turbines. They generate electricity when the wind does not blow.

People use wind for different things. Wind sails boats. Windmills grind grain. They pump water from the ground and farmers use the water for their crops. A windmill can power a saw. People use the saw to cut lumber for building.

People in early America used windmills to crush ore. Windmills churned butter. They pumped water for indoor plumbing.

Some people think wind farms take up a lot of space. Farmers can grow crops on the land below wind turbines. Other people say wind farms are too noisy. They think wind farms block the view. Wind farms out in the ocean do not bother anyone.

Wind power is safe and clean. It does not cause pollution. It takes no fuel to run a wind turbine. California has wind farms. They provide one-third of the world's wind power. People are thinking about using more wind power.

Wind Power

Directions: Darken the best answer choice.

1. At the least, how fast should the wind blow to power a wind turbine?
   Ⓐ sixty miles per hour
   Ⓑ eleven miles per hour
   Ⓒ thirty-one miles per hour
   Ⓓ thirteen miles per minute

2. A **generator** produces electricity by
   Ⓐ turning a magnet inside a coil of wire.
   Ⓑ standing in the wind.
   Ⓒ sending water through a tunnel.
   Ⓓ sitting in the sun.

3. What happens after water is released from a high lake or reservoir?
   Ⓐ It flows down a tunnel and turns a turbine.
   Ⓑ The wind does not blow.
   Ⓒ The water moves to a higher place.
   Ⓓ Extra power pumps water from a low lake.

4. What makes the wind blow?
   Ⓐ blades of a windmill turning in the air
   Ⓑ rain falling from clouds
   Ⓒ high air pressure moving to be equal with low air pressure
   Ⓓ ocean waves crashing on shore

5. Which place provides one-third of the world's wind power?
   Ⓐ Europe
   Ⓑ Persia
   Ⓒ California
   Ⓓ Egypt

6. Picture a windmill. What is one thing it *cannot* do?
   Ⓐ grind grain
   Ⓑ pump water
   Ⓒ churn butter
   Ⓓ sail a boat

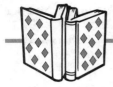

Komodo Dragons

Do you like dragons? Would you like to meet one? Many zoos have a dragon. It is a reptile. We call it a Komodo dragon.

Komodo dragons are big lizards! Their tails are longer than their bodies. They look like small tanks. They have long, flat heads. Their legs are bowed.

Reptiles have skin with scales. So do Komodo dragons. They are cold-blooded. They lie in the sun to get warm.

Dragons eat many things. They like deer best. They also eat pigs and other dead animals. They may eat other dragons. Dragons may even eat people!

Komodo dragons hunt alone. They bite their prey. Dragons have a weak bite. But they have sharp teeth. The bite might not kill the victim. The dragon waits. Dragon **saliva** has many germs. It harms the victim. Animals may escape the dragon's bite. But they will die from the germs.

Dragons live in hot forests. They roam in grasslands. They live on islands in the ocean.

Dragons have no enemies. They hide and wait for prey. Dragons can run fast. They can swim well.

Adult dragons may eat dragon babies. The young get away. They climb trees. Baby dragons eat insects and geckos.

Komodo dragons are in danger. Humans destroy their forests. People hunt the dragons' food. We hope dragons will be here for a long time!

Komodo Dragons

Do you like dragons? Would you like to meet one? Many zoos have a dragon. It is a reptile. We call it a Komodo dragon.

Komodo dragons are the world's biggest lizards! Their tails are longer than their bodies. Komodo dragons look like small tanks. They have long, flat heads. Their legs are bowed.

Like other reptiles, Komodo dragons have scaly skin. They are cold-blooded. They like to lie in the sun to get warm.

Dragons eat many things. Their favorite food is deer. They also prey on pigs and other dead animals. They often eat other dragons. Dragons may even eat people!

Komodo dragons hunt alone. They bite their prey with sharp teeth. Dragons have a weak bite. It might not kill the victim. The dragon follows and waits. Dragon **saliva** has many germs. It poisons the victim. Animals can escape the dragon's bite. But they will die soon from blood poisoning.

The dragons live on islands in Indonesia. They live in tropical forests. They roam in grasslands, too.

Dragons have no enemies. They hide and wait for prey. Dragons can run fast for a short time. They can swim well.

Adult dragons eat baby dragons. The young climb trees to escape. Baby dragons eat eggs, insects, and geckos.

Komodo dragons are in danger. Humans destroy their habitat. People also hunt their food. We hope dragons will be here for a long time!

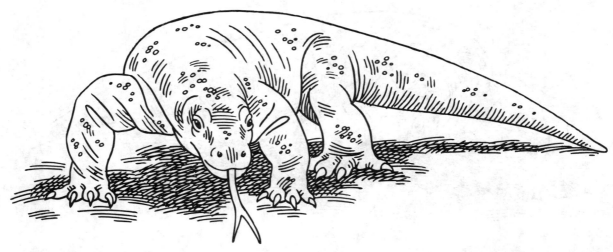

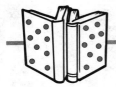

Komodo Dragons

Do you like dragons? Would you like to meet one? Many zoos have a dragon. It is called a Komodo dragon.

Komodo dragons are the world's largest lizards! Their muscular tails are longer than their bodies. Dragons look like small tanks. They have long, flat heads. Their legs are bowed.

Like all reptiles, they have scaly skin and are cold-blooded. They lie in the sun to get warm.

Dragons eat almost anything. They eat deer, pigs, water buffalo, and other dead animals. They also eat other dragons and even people.

Komodo dragons hunt alone. They bite their prey with their sharp teeth. The bite does not always kill the victim. The dragon follows and waits. Dragon **saliva** has many germs. It poisons the victim. Animals can escape the Komodo dragon's bite. But they will die within twenty-four hours from blood poisoning.

The dragons live on islands in Indonesia. Hot grasslands and tropical forests make up their habitat.

Dragons have no enemies. Camouflage allows them to hide. Dragons run fast in short bursts. They swim well.

Young Komodo dragons fall prey to adult dragons. Young dragons climb trees to escape being eaten. Baby dragons eat eggs, beetles, grasshoppers, and geckos.

Komodo dragons are endangered. Humans destroy their habitat. They kill food that dragons eat. We hope dragons will be here for a long time!

Komodo Dragons

Directions: Darken the best answer choice.

1. Where do Komodo dragons live?
   - Ⓐ in the mountains
   - Ⓑ on islands
   - Ⓒ by a river
   - Ⓓ in lakes

2. A dragon's **saliva** is
   - Ⓐ a spear it throws at animals.
   - Ⓑ the clear liquid in its mouth.
   - Ⓒ what it eats.
   - Ⓓ a horn on its head.

3. What happens first?
   - Ⓐ The dragon waits.
   - Ⓑ The bite victim is harmed.
   - Ⓒ The bite victim dies.
   - Ⓓ A Komodo dragon bites its victim.

4. Young Komodo dragons climb trees to
   - Ⓐ escape being eaten by adult dragons.
   - Ⓑ have fun with each other.
   - Ⓒ see if a wild pig is chasing them.
   - Ⓓ eat leaves and fruit.

5. Why do we call this reptile a dragon?
   - Ⓐ It breathes fire.
   - Ⓑ It has wings.
   - Ⓒ It has sharp teeth and tears apart its food.
   - Ⓓ It can fly.

6. Picture a young Komodo dragon. It is
   - Ⓐ in a tree.
   - Ⓑ in the ocean.
   - Ⓒ in the army.
   - Ⓓ in the shade.

The Sounds We Hear

We hear sounds all around us. Some noises are louder than others. Our ears send messages to our brains. They tell us where sounds come from. The messages tell our brain what the sounds mean.

Noise creates sound waves. They travel through the air. Sound waves enter the outer ear. They travel down the ear canal. Then, they get to the eardrum. The sound waves make the eardrum move. Sound energy goes to the middle ear.

The middle ear has three bones. Sound hits the hammer first. It moves against the anvil. The anvil passes the vibrations along. It hits the stirrup. Sound waves are sent along.

Next, the cochlea gets the sound waves. It is shaped like a snail. It is full of fluid. The cochlea has tiny hairs. Sound waves move the hairs. Then, they touch membranes.

There is a nerve in the ear. It makes a nerve impulse. The nerve impulse travels to the brain. The brain understands this impulse as sound.

We measure sound in **decibels**. Decibels tell the loudness of a sound. Sound waves have force when they hit the ear. Talking is fifty to sixty decibels. A jet engine measures 130–160 decibels.

Many kids have hearing loss. It comes from loud noise. There are things you can do to protect your ears. Turn down music when you listen to it. Walk away from loud noises. If you are by loud machines, wear earplugs.

Save your hearing. Protect your ears. You will keep hearing all the sounds you enjoy for a long time.

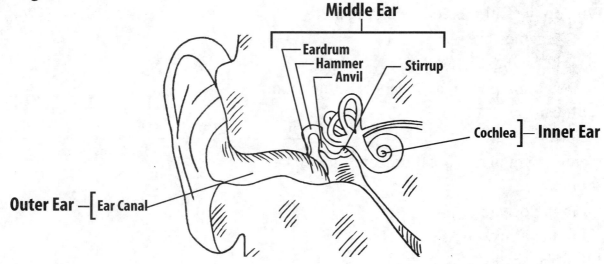

The Sounds We Hear

We hear sounds all around us. Some noises are louder than others. Our ears send messages to our brains. The messages tell us where sounds come from. Our brain interprets the sounds.

Noise creates sound waves. The sound waves travel through the air. They enter the outer ear. They travel down the ear canal to the eardrum. The sound waves vibrate the eardrum. This sends the sound energy to the middle ear.

The middle ear has three bones. Sound waves hit the hammer first. It moves against the anvil and passes the vibrations along. The anvil hits the stirrup. Sound waves are sent along.

Next, the cochlea receives the vibrations. The cochlea is shaped like a snail. It is full of fluid. Tiny hairs in the cochlea move with the sound waves. The tiny hairs touch membranes.

The auditory nerve generates a nerve impulse. The nerve impulse travels to the brain. The brain understands this impulse as sound.

We measure sound in **decibels**. Decibels indicate the loudness of a sound and how much force sound waves have when they hit the ear. For example, talking is fifty to sixty decibels. A jet engine is 130–160 decibels.

More and more kids have hearing loss from loud noise. There are things you can do to protect your ears. Turn down music when you listen to it. Walk away from loud noises. If you are by loud machines, wear earplugs.

Protecting your ears saves your hearing. You will keep hearing all the sounds you enjoy for a long time.

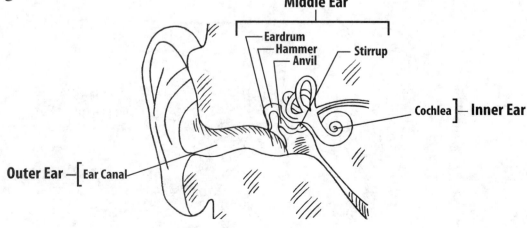

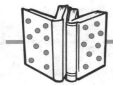

The Sounds We Hear

We hear sounds all around us. Some noises are louder than others. Our ears send messages to our brains. The messages tell us where sounds come from. Our brain interprets the sounds.

Noise creates vibrations called sound waves. The sound waves travel through the air. Sound waves enter the outer ear. They travel down the ear canal to the eardrum. The sound waves vibrate the eardrum. This sends the sound energy to the middle ear.

The middle ear has three bones. Sound waves hit the hammer first. It vibrates against the anvil and passes the sound waves along. The anvil hits the stirrup and passes the vibrations to the inner ear.

Next, the cochlea receives the vibrations. The cochlea is shaped like a snail and is full of fluid. Tiny hairs in the cochlea vibrate with the sound waves. The tiny hairs touch membranes.

The auditory nerve generates a nerve impulse. The nerve impulse travels to the brain. The brain understands this impulse as sound.

We measure sound in **decibels**. Decibels indicate the loudness of a sound and how much force sound waves have when they hit the ear. For example, talking is fifty to sixty decibels. A jet engine measures 130–160 decibels. Loud music is 115 decibels.

More and more kids have hearing loss from loud noise. There are things you can do to protect your ears. Turn down music when you listen to it. Walk away from loud noises. If you are by loud machines, wear ear protection.

Protecting your ears saves your hearing. Your ears will enable you to hear the sounds around you for many years.

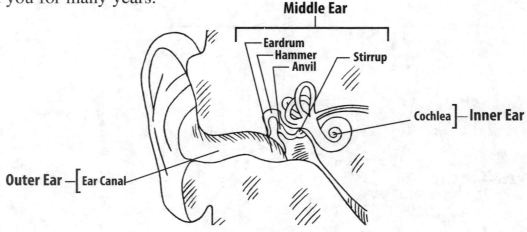

The Sounds We Hear

Directions: Darken the best answer choice.

1. Which bone is shaped like a snail?
   - Ⓐ the cochlea
   - Ⓑ the hammer
   - Ⓒ the anvil
   - Ⓓ the stirrup

2. **Decibels** measure
   - Ⓐ the length of sound waves.
   - Ⓑ the size of your ears.
   - Ⓒ the loudness of sounds.
   - Ⓓ the number of bells you hear.

3. What happens last?
   - Ⓐ Sound waves enter the ear.
   - Ⓑ A nerve impulse travels to the brain.
   - Ⓒ The anvil hits the stirrup.
   - Ⓓ The eardrum vibrates.

4. What causes hearing loss?
   - Ⓐ tiny hairs
   - Ⓑ earplugs
   - Ⓒ loud noise
   - Ⓓ swimming

5. How do we hear sound?
   - Ⓐ Our brain receives a nerve impulse.
   - Ⓑ We pick up a snail shell.
   - Ⓒ Our friends talk.
   - Ⓓ We play the eardrum.

6. Sound waves enter the
   - Ⓐ nose.
   - Ⓑ mouth.
   - Ⓒ eye.
   - Ⓓ ear.

Find Your Way

A map shows details of an area. People use maps to find places.

Maps have directions. A compass rose is a picture. The picture stands for a compass. It is on the side of a map. Letters stand for each direction.

A **compass** is a tool. It helps people find directions. A needle points towards the North Pole. It has a magnet in it. The *N* on the picture faces the same way as the north on a map.

Globes are round. They are models of Earth. It would be hard to take a globe with you. Mapmakers show Earth on flat paper. People go up in the air. They take pictures of Earth. This helps them make maps more correct.

Grids help people find something on a map. A grid has lines going across. Lines also go up and down. The lines form columns and rows. Look at the lines going across. They have letters. Look at the lines going down. They have numbers. Use your fingers. Trace the lines for a letter and a number. Look at the point where your fingers come together. Name the place that is in that square of the grid.

There are different kinds of maps. Physical maps show things in nature. They show land and water. Physical maps also show landforms. They show lakes and rivers. They show mountain ranges.

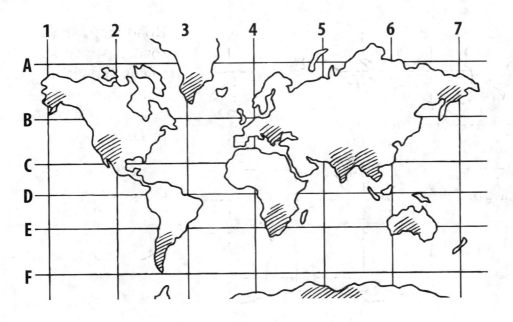

Road maps show roads. They show towns and cities. People read the map. They learn how to get from one place to another.

Maps help us see things beyond where we are. We use them to go places. Use a map to show a friend how to find your house.

Find Your Way

A map shows details of an area. People use maps to find places.

People use maps for many reasons. Maps show roads and places. They help people get from one place to another.

Maps have directions. A compass rose is a picture on the side of a map. The picture stands for a compass. It has letters to stand for each direction.

A **compass** is an instrument. It helps people find directions. A magnetic needle points towards the North Pole. The *N* on the picture faces the same direction as the north on a map.

Globes are round models of Earth. It would be difficult to take a globe with you. Mapmakers have to figure out how to show features of Earth on flat paper. People take pictures of Earth from the air. This helps them make maps more accurate.

Grids help people locate something on a map. A grid has lines going across and up and down. The lines form columns and rows. The lines going across have letters. The lines going down have numbers. Use your fingers to trace a letter and a number. Look at the point where your fingers come together. Name the place that is in that square of the grid.

There are different kinds of maps. Physical maps show natural objects. They show areas of land and water. Physical maps also show landforms. They show lakes and rivers. They show mountains.

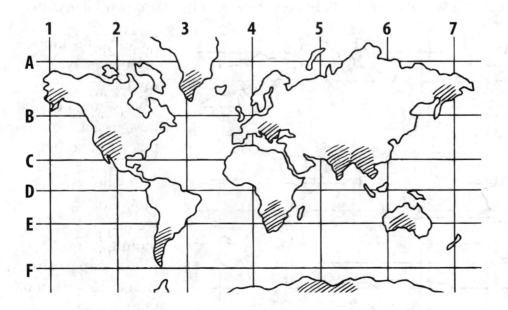

Road maps show roads, as well as towns and cities. They show people how to get from one place to another.

Maps help us see things beyond where we are. We use them to go places. Use a map to show a friend how to find your house.

Find Your Way

Maps show details and features of an area. People use maps to find various places.

People use maps for many reasons. They use them to travel from one place to another.

Maps have directions. A compass rose is a picture on the side of a map with letters to stand for each direction.

The picture stands for a **compass**, an instrument that helps people to find directions. A magnetic needle points towards the North Pole. The *N* on the picture faces the same direction as the north on a map.

Globes are round models of Earth. It would be difficult to take a globe with you. Cartographers make maps. They have to figure out how to show features of Earth on flat paper. Mapmakers take pictures of Earth from the air. This helps them make maps more accurate.

Grids help people locate certain places on a map. A grid has lines going across and up and down. The lines form columns and rows. The lines going across have letters or numbers. The lines going down have numbers. Use your fingers to trace along a letter and a number. Look at the point where your fingers come together. Name the place that is in that square of the grid.

There are different kinds of maps. Physical maps show natural objects such as land and water. Physical maps also show landforms like lakes, rivers, mountains, and canyons.

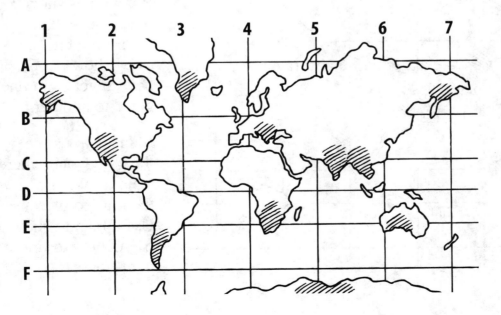

Road maps show highways, roads, towns, and cities. They show people how to get from one place to another.

Maps help us see things beyond where we are. We use them to go places. Use a map to show a friend how to find your house.

Find Your Way

Directions: Darken the best answer choice.

1. Where is the compass rose?
   - Ⓐ in a garden
   - Ⓑ on a ship
   - Ⓒ on the side of a map
   - Ⓓ on a globe

2. A **compass** has
   - Ⓐ a magnetic needle that points north.
   - Ⓑ a special needle that points south.
   - Ⓒ a tool in the shed.
   - Ⓓ a flower that folds up.

3. What is the last thing you do when you look for a place on a map grid?
   - Ⓐ Look at the lines going across.
   - Ⓑ Look at the point where your fingers come together.
   - Ⓒ Look at the lines going down.
   - Ⓓ Trace a number and a letter with your fingers.

4. How is a globe different from a map?
   - Ⓐ A globe shows land on Earth.
   - Ⓑ A globe shows oceans.
   - Ⓒ A globe is smaller than a map.
   - Ⓓ A globe is round.

5. What is one way to make a map more accurate?
   - Ⓐ Walk to all the places.
   - Ⓑ Take pictures from the air.
   - Ⓒ Draw pictures of animals.
   - Ⓓ Face the North Pole.

6. Picture a road map. What is *not* on it?
   - Ⓐ rain
   - Ⓑ roads
   - Ⓒ towns
   - Ⓓ cities

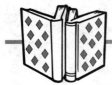

Let's Play

We all have places we enjoy. Perhaps you like the playground best. A playground is a place to play. A playground is free. It might be at your school.

Many parks have playgrounds. They have things to play on. Most have swings and slides. Children climb on jungle gyms. There might be seesaws. Some playgrounds have other things. Some have monkey bars. There might be bridges. There might be playhouses.

Younger children play in sandboxes. There might be tunnels. Children climb on poles. They jump rope. Other countries have playgrounds, too. They have the same kinds of play things.

Russian playgrounds have small merry-go-rounds. They call them carousels. There are climbing gyms. They are in the shape of large spheres. They have walking bridges.

In Asian countries, people want children to learn. They think it is good for children to learn when they play. They also want children to be safe.

Playgrounds in Iceland have places for skateboards. They have castles in which to play.

Africa has seven special playgrounds. They make electricity. Children ride the merry-go-rounds. As they turn, they make electricity. They use the light to read at night.

A place in the United States makes playgrounds. People work there. They think of new ideas. They put fountains in some playgrounds. Children play in the water. Some fountains have music. Playgrounds could have **prisms** that bend light into many colors. They might have mirrors.

Think about the playground you like best. How can you make it better? You can pick up trash. You can play safely. You can help others enjoy the playground.

Let's Play

We all have special places we enjoy. Perhaps you like the playground best. A playground is a place to play. A playground is free. It might be at your school.

Many parks have playgrounds. They have things to play on. Most have swings and slides. Children climb on jungle gyms. There might be seesaws. Some playgrounds have monkey bars. There might be walking bridges or playhouses.

Playgrounds for younger children have sandboxes. There might be tunnels. Children climb on poles or play jump rope. Other countries have playgrounds, too. They have the same kinds of things on which to play.

Russian playgrounds have metal equipment. They have small merry-go-rounds. They call them carousels. The climbing gyms are in the shape of large spheres. They have walking bridges.

In Asian countries, people want children to learn things when they play. They also want children to be safe.

In Iceland, playgrounds have a place for skateboards. They have castles in which to play.

Seven playgrounds in Africa make electricity. When children ride the merry-go-rounds, they make electricity. They use the light to study at night.

A company in the United States makes playgrounds. People who work there think of new ideas. They thought of having fountains in playgrounds. Children could play in the water. Some fountains would have music. They thought of ways to play with light. Playgrounds could have mirrors or **prisms** that bend light into many colors.

Think about the playground you like best. How can you make it better? You can pick up trash. You can play safely. You can help others enjoy the playground.

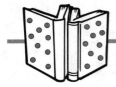

Let's Play

We all have special places we enjoy. Perhaps your favorite place is the playground. A playground is a place where children can play freely. Your school might have a playground.

Many parks have playgrounds. They have play equipment. Most have swings and slides. Children climb on jungle gyms. There might be seesaws. Some playgrounds have monkey bars. There might be walking bridges or playhouses.

Playgrounds for younger children have sandboxes. There might be tunnels. Children climb on poles or play jump rope. Other countries have playgrounds, too. They have the same kinds of play equipment.

Playgrounds in Russia have metal equipment. They have small merry-go-rounds called carousels. The climbing gyms are in the shape of large spheres. They have walking bridges.

In Asian countries, people want children to learn things when they play. They also want children to be safe.

In Iceland, playgrounds have a place for skateboards. They have castles in which to play.

Seven playgrounds in Africa make electricity. When children ride the merry-go-rounds, they make electricity. They use the light to study at night.

A company in the United States makes playgrounds. People who work there think of new ideas. They thought of having interactive fountains in playgrounds. Children could play in the water. Some fountains would have music. They thought of ways to play with light. Playgrounds could have mirrors or **prisms** that bend light into many colors.

Think about the playground you like best. How can you make it better? You can pick up litter. You can play safely. You can help others enjoy the playground.

Let's Play

Directions: Darken the best answer choice.

1. Which country has playgrounds with carousels?

   Ⓐ Asia

   Ⓑ Russia

   Ⓒ Iceland

   Ⓓ United States

2. **Prisms** are glass shapes that

   Ⓐ bend light into colors of the rainbow.

   Ⓑ float in water.

   Ⓒ look like a castle.

   Ⓓ have light and a mirror.

3. What happens last?

   Ⓐ Children ride the merry-go-round.

   Ⓑ The merry-go-round turns.

   Ⓒ Children use the light to read at night.

   Ⓓ The merry-go-round makes electricity.

4. How are playgrounds in Iceland different from other playgrounds in this story?

   Ⓐ They have music.

   Ⓑ They have a sandbox.

   Ⓒ They have castles.

   Ⓓ They have a sphere.

5. Why do playgrounds in Africa make electricity?

   Ⓐ So children can ride a merry-go-round.

   Ⓑ So grown-ups can have a job.

   Ⓒ So children can have new playgrounds.

   Ⓓ So children can read at night.

6. *None* of the playgrounds in this story have

   Ⓐ slides.

   Ⓑ computers.

   Ⓒ swings.

   Ⓓ bridges.

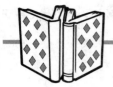

Deserts

Deserts are hot and dry. How can anything live in a desert? Deserts cover one-fifth of Earth.

Deserts have dry air. Water **evaporates** quickly. It changes to water vapor. Sometimes it starts to rain. The rain dries up before it hits the ground. A hot, dry desert gets over 100°F. It cools down at night to about 50°F.

Hot, dry deserts do not get much rain. Rain falls all at once. This downpour makes it flood. Then, it doesn't rain for a long time. In a desert, less than ten inches of rain falls a year.

Cold deserts are near the Arctic. They have warm summers. Temperatures are around 80°F. It can get as warm as 100°F. It cools down at night. Summers are short. Snow falls in the winter. Sometimes it rains in the spring. It is still a desert. Less than ten inches of rain or snow falls a year.

Desert plants store water. They go a long time without water. They can stand hot weather. Plants do not grow very tall. Their leaves have spines. This reduces water loss. Sagebrush grows in cold deserts. It gives shade to plants. Plants grow taller in cold deserts.

Desert animals are active at night. They burrow during the day. Animals get water from their food. They eat seeds and plant leaves. Some animals eat small animals and insects. Animals are the same color as the desert sand. This protects them from enemies.

Kangaroo rats live in deserts. Jackrabbits and grasshoppers also live in deserts. Camels live in hot deserts. Antelope live in cold deserts.

Not all deserts are hot. But most are dry. Plants and animals have found ways to live in deserts.

42

Deserts

Deserts are hot and dry. How can anything survive in a desert? Deserts cover one-fifth of Earth's surface.

Deserts have low humidity. Water **evaporates** quickly and changes to water vapor. When it does start to rain, the rain evaporates before it hits the ground. A hot, dry desert gets over 100°F. It cools down at night to about 50°F.

Hot, dry deserts do not get much rain. Rain falls all at once. This downpour makes it flood. Then, it doesn't rain for a long time. In a desert, less than ten inches of rain falls a year.

Cold deserts are near the Arctic. They have short, warm summers. Temperatures are around 80°F. But they can get as warm as 100°F. It cools down at night. Snow falls in the winter. Sometimes it rains in the spring. These deserts still get less than ten inches of rain or snow each year.

Desert plants store water for long periods of time. They can stand hot weather. Plants do not grow very tall. Their leaves have spines. This reduces water loss. Sagebrush grows in cold deserts. It provides shade for other plants. Plants grow taller in cold deserts.

Desert animals are active at night. They burrow during the day. Animals get water from their food. They eat seeds and plant leaves. Some animals eat small animals and insects. Camouflage protects animals from predators.

Kangaroo rats live in deserts. Camels live in hot deserts. Jackrabbits and grasshoppers also live in deserts. Antelope live in cold deserts.

Not all deserts are hot. But most are dry. Plants and animals have found ways to survive in deserts.

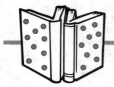

Deserts

Deserts are hot and dry. We wonder how anything can survive in a desert. Deserts cover one-fifth of land on Earth.

Deserts have low humidity. Water **evaporates** quickly and changes to water vapor. When it does start to rain, the rain evaporates before it hits the ground. A hot, dry desert reaches temperatures of over 100°F in the summer. The temperature at night is about 50°F.

Hot, dry deserts do not get much rain. Rain falls in a downpour, and the sudden rain causes flooding. Then, it doesn't rain for a long time. In a desert, less than ten inches of rain falls a year.

There are also cold deserts. These deserts are near the Arctic. They have short, warm summers. Temperatures are around 80°F. It can get as warm as 100°F, but it cools down at night. Snow falls in the winter, and sometimes it rains in the spring. These deserts still get less than ten inches of rain or snow each year.

Desert plants store water for long periods of time. They can stand the hot weather. Plants do not grow very tall. They have spiny leaves to reduce water loss. Sagebrush grows in cold deserts. It provides shade for other plants. Plants grow taller in cold deserts.

Desert animals are active at night. They burrow during the day. Animals get water from the food they eat. They eat seeds, plant leaves, or other small animals and insects. Camouflage protects animals from predators.

Kangaroo rats live in hot, dry deserts. Camels live in hot deserts. Jackrabbits and grasshoppers also live in deserts. Antelope live in cold deserts.

Not all deserts are hot. But most are dry. Plants and animals have found ways to survive in deserts.

Deserts

Directions: Darken the best answer choice.

1. What falls in a cold desert?
   - Ⓐ snow
   - Ⓑ hail
   - Ⓒ clouds
   - Ⓓ leaves

2. When water **evaporates**, it changes to
   - Ⓐ rain.
   - Ⓑ dust.
   - Ⓒ water vapor.
   - Ⓓ ice.

3. What happens after the sun goes down?
   - Ⓐ It gets hot.
   - Ⓑ Animals go to bed.
   - Ⓒ Plants grow taller.
   - Ⓓ Animals are active.

4. How are hot and cold deserts alike?
   - Ⓐ They have tall trees.
   - Ⓑ They do not get much rain.
   - Ⓒ They have camels.
   - Ⓓ They are near the Arctic.

5. The warmest a desert gets is
   - Ⓐ about 50°F.
   - Ⓑ over 100°F.
   - Ⓒ less than 10°F.
   - Ⓓ up to 80°F.

6. Picture a desert. What is *not* there?
   - Ⓐ a lake
   - Ⓑ sand
   - Ⓒ jackrabbits
   - Ⓓ sagebrush

The Biggest Waves

Waves pound the shore. Some people like to watch the waves. Some people fear the ocean waves. We call huge waves tsunamis.

The huge waves are long. They move across the ocean. They move very fast. They travel over 450 mph. The waves hit land. They are over fifty feet high.

Earthquakes can take place under the ocean. Sometimes the ocean floor **tilts**. This makes huge waves we call tsunamis. A volcano erupts. It also causes waves.

These waves move in all ways. It is like dropping a pebble in a pond. Waves move across the water.

Huge waves have a lot of water. They have energy. Waves hit the shore. They cause damage. Huge waves can hurt a town.

The first big wave hits the shore. It makes a wave lower than sea level. People can get away. Then, the waves get larger.

A tsunami starts in the ocean. There are many volcanoes. They cause earthquakes. Huge waves hit Hawaii almost every year. They also hit Alaska.

Sometimes people drown in the huge waves. Water floods the land. The waves pollute drinking water.

Some areas have ways to warn people. The warning center scans the ocean. It looks for changes. It looks for things that cause huge waves. People can get away. They escape from huge waves. They need to know where to go. They can go to a high place. The warning tells people when to go.

The Biggest Waves

Waves pound the shore. Some people like to watch the waves. Some people fear the ocean waves. We call huge waves tsunamis.

The huge waves are long. They move across the ocean. They move very fast. They travel over 450 mph. The waves are over fifty feet high when they hit land.

Earthquakes can take place under the ocean. Sometimes the ocean floor **tilts**. This makes huge waves we call tsunamis. A volcano erupts. It also causes waves.

These waves move in all directions. It is like dropping a pebble in a pond. Ripples travel across the water.

Huge waves have a lot of water. They have a lot of energy. Waves hit the shore. They cause damage. A tsunami can hurt a town.

The first big wave hits the shore. It makes a wave lower than sea level. People might have time to escape. Then, the waves get larger.

Tsunamis happen in the Pacific Ocean. There are many volcanoes. Earthquakes happen often. Huge waves hit Hawaii almost every year. They also hit Alaska.

Sometimes people drown in the huge waves. Water floods the land. The waves pollute drinking water.

Some areas have warning systems. The warning center tracks changes in the ocean. It looks for things that cause huge waves. People can get away from big waves. They need to know where to go. They can go to higher ground. The warning tells people when to escape.

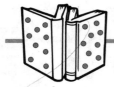

The Biggest Waves

Crashing waves pound the shore. For some people, watching the ocean is exciting. Other people fear ocean waves. We call huge waves tsunamis.

Tsunamis move across the ocean. They are long and they move fast. They travel over 450 mph. These waves reach fifty to one hundred feet high when they hit land.

Earthquakes can happen under the ocean. They cause tsunamis. Sometimes the ocean floor **tilts**. Huge waves are created. This can also happen when a volcano erupts.

These waves travel in all directions. It is like dropping a pebble in a pond. Ripples move across the water.

The waves have large amounts of water. They have a lot of energy. When they hit the shore, they can cause great damage. A tsunami can destroy a town.

A tsunami hits the shore. It creates a wave lower than sea level. This often gives people time to escape. Then, the waves get larger again.

Most tsunamis happen in the Pacific Ocean. This ocean has many volcanoes. Earthquakes happen often. Hawaii is hit by huge waves almost every year. So is Alaska.

Sometimes people drown in huge waves. Water floods the land. The waves pollute the water people drink.

Some areas have warning systems. The warning center tracks disturbances in the ocean. It looks for things that could cause huge waves. People need to know where to go if a tsunami hits. They can go to higher ground. The warning system tells people when to escape.

The Biggest Waves

Directions: Darken the best answer choice.

1. Tsunamis hit Hawaii
   Ⓐ every day.
   Ⓑ when it rains.
   Ⓒ almost every year.
   Ⓓ in the summer.

2. When the ocean floor **tilts**
   Ⓐ water turns around.
   Ⓑ it leans to one side.
   Ⓒ a mountain grows.
   Ⓓ it dries up.

3. What happens first?
   Ⓐ People get a warning.
   Ⓑ Large waves hit the shore.
   Ⓒ Water floods the land.
   Ⓓ People go to a high place.

4. A tsunami is like
   Ⓐ dropping a pebble in a pond.
   Ⓑ giving a warning.
   Ⓒ rowing a boat.
   Ⓓ watching the seashore.

5. If a tsunami comes, people should
   Ⓐ stay and watch.
   Ⓑ swim to safety.
   Ⓒ go to a high place.
   Ⓓ wait for the next wave.

6. Picture a tsunami. The wave is
   Ⓐ as big as a person.
   Ⓑ as tall as a five-story building.
   Ⓒ as big as the whole ocean.
   Ⓓ as fast as a car.

The Shape of the Land

Have you ever flown in a plane? You can see the land below. It is not all the same. You can see different shapes. There are high places and low places. You might see water. We call these landforms.

Glaciers are moving sheets of ice. They slide slowly across rock. The ice leaves grooves in the rock.

Weather and water change land. Wind blows across sand. The dunes change shape. The sand has ridges. Water wears away dirt. It wears down rock. Riverbanks get wider. They change shape.

Mountains and hills are common landforms. Some mountains have flat tops. They are mesas. They have steep sides. Mesa means table. Some people call these "tablelands." The western United States has tablelands.

A valley lies between two mountains. A canyon is a deep valley. It is narrow. There is a river at the bottom. It has steep sides. The Grand Canyon is in Arizona. The steep rock sides form cliffs.

A river flows through most valleys. Some valleys are dry. They might have a gulch. A gulch fills with water only when it rains. Other valleys have mighty rivers. The Columbia River has a lot of water. It has cut a gorge. A gorge is a deep valley. It has steep, rocky sides. Some gorges are narrow. Water wears down the rock sides over time.

A volcano is a mountain that changes. It has vents. Steam and lava escape. When it erupts, it affects the land around it. The eruption throws out chunks of rock and ash. Hummocks are low hills. They are made of **debris** from the volcano.

When landforms change, it affects our lives. We study landforms. We want to know how the changes will affect us.

The Shape of the Land

Have you ever flown in an airplane and looked at the land below? It is not all the same. You can see different shapes. There are high places and low places. You might see water. We call these things landforms.

Glaciers are moving sheets of ice. A glacier slides slowly across rock. It leaves grooves in the rock.

Weather and water change land. Wind blows across the sand. The dunes change shape. The sand has ridges in it. Water wears away dirt and rock. Over time, riverbanks get wider. They change shape.

Mountains, hills, and plains are common landforms. Other landforms we do not hear about as often. A mountain with steep sides and a flat top is a mesa. Mesa means table. Some people call this landform "tablelands." There are tablelands in the western United States.

A valley lies between two hills or mountains. A deep, narrow river valley with steep sides is a canyon. The Grand Canyon is in Arizona. The steep rock sides form cliffs.

Most valleys have a river flowing through them. Some valleys are dry. A gulch fills with water only when it rains. Other valleys have mighty rivers. The Columbia River has a lot of water. It has cut a gorge. A gorge is a deep valley with steep, rocky sides. Some gorges are very narrow. Water wears down the rock sides over time.

A volcano is a mountain that changes. It has vents. Steam and lava escape. When a volcano erupts, it affects the land around it. The eruption throws out chunks of rock and ash. Hummocks are low hills that are made of **debris** from the volcano.

When landforms change, it makes a difference in our lives. We study landforms to understand how these changes will affect us.

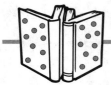

The Shape of the Land

Have you ever flown in an airplane and looked at the land below? It is not all the same. You can see different shapes, high places, and low places. You might see water. We call these things landforms. Each landform has its own characteristics.

Glaciers are moving sheets of ice that slide slowly across rock, leaving ridges or grooves in the land.

Weather and water change land. Wind blows across the sand. The dunes change shape. The sand has ridges in it. Water wears away dirt and rock. Over time, riverbanks get wider or change shape.

Mountains, hills, plains, rivers, and lakes are common landforms. Other landforms we do not hear about as often. A hill or a mountain with steep sides and a flat top is a mesa. Mesa means table. Some people call this landform "tablelands." There are tablelands in the western United States.

A valley lies between two hills or mountains. A deep, narrow river valley with steep sides is a canyon. You may have heard of the Grand Canyon in Arizona. The steep rock sides form cliffs.

Most valleys have a river flowing through them. A gulch is a valley that fills with water only when it rains. Other valleys have mighty rivers. The Columbia River has so much water that it has cut a gorge. A gorge is a deep valley with steep, rocky sides, worn away over time. Some gorges are very narrow.

A volcano is a mountain that changes. It has vents through which steam and lava escape. When a volcano erupts, it affects the land around it. The eruption throws chunks of rock and ash out of the mountain. Hummocks are low hills that are made of volcanic **debris**.

When landforms change, it affects people's lives. We study landforms to understand how these changes will affect us.

The Shape of the Land

Directions: Darken the best answer choice.

1. What is a glacier?
   - Ⓐ an ice-cream cone
   - Ⓑ a moving sheet of ice
   - Ⓒ a rock with grooves
   - Ⓓ a river in a valley

2. Hummocks have **debris** from a volcano. They have
   - Ⓐ scattered pieces of rock and ash.
   - Ⓑ stuff from a garage sale.
   - Ⓒ sheets of ice.
   - Ⓓ steep, rocky sides.

3. What happens in a gulch after it rains?
   - Ⓐ The gulch becomes dry.
   - Ⓑ It erupts with lava.
   - Ⓒ Sheets of ice appear.
   - Ⓓ It fills with water.

4. What is most like a gorge?
   - Ⓐ a mountain
   - Ⓑ a canyon
   - Ⓒ a glacier
   - Ⓓ a sand dune

5. Why are mesas called "tablelands"?
   - Ⓐ They have food on them.
   - Ⓑ They have four legs.
   - Ⓒ They are flat on top.
   - Ⓓ They are in the United States.

6. Picture a canyon. What will you *not* see?
   - Ⓐ a river way down at the bottom
   - Ⓑ a flat, grassy meadow
   - Ⓒ cliffs
   - Ⓓ steep, rocky sides

Money

Long ago, people traded to buy things. They traded animals. They got food. Then, they traded food to get other things.

People did things for others. They traded shells. They traded beads. They even traded furs.

People wanted a better way to trade for things. They used coins. The coins were bronze. Coins had value. People spent coins. They bought things.

People called this money. They used gold. Sometimes they had silver. Each coin was worth some gold or silver.

After awhile, the United States made paper money. People copied it. They made fake money. Ben Franklin did not like this. He made bills with pictures.

Congress passed a law. It set the worth of a coin. The law based the value on gold. Some coins had worth in silver. Some had worth in copper. A mint first made coins in 1793.

Later, the U.S. printed paper money again. They called it "greenbacks." Can you guess its color?

Printers added things to paper money. They had fine lines cut in it. It has numbers on it that tell how much it is worth.

The government added a **seal** to paper money. The seal is a design.

Someone signed money. Later, they added color to notes. Then, they added special thread. These things make it hard to copy money.

Today, people also use credit cards. They use ATM cards. People do not carry as many coins.

Money

Long ago, people traded to buy things. They traded animals and food. They traded what they had.

They had people do things for them. They traded shells. They traded beads or stones. They even traded furs.

People wanted a better way to trade for things. They used bronze coins. Coins had value. Everyone wanted coins. They spent coins to get things.

People called this money. They used gold. Sometimes they used silver or paper. Money was worth an amount. Each coin was worth so much gold.

One of the colonies issued the first paper money. People copied the money. They made fake money. Ben Franklin did not like this. He made bills with nature prints.

Congress passed a law. It said how much a coin was worth. The law based the value on gold, silver, or copper. A mint made the first coins in 1793.

Later, the U.S. printed paper money again. People called it "greenbacks." Can you guess its color?

The government added things to paper money. It had fine lines cut in it. It had numbers on it that told how much it is worth.

The government added a **seal** to paper money. The seal is a design.

Every note had a signature. Printers added color to notes. Later, they added special thread. These things make it hard to copy money.

Today, people also use credit cards. They use ATM cards. People do not carry as much cash.

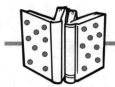

Money

In the past, people traded to buy things. They traded animals and food. They traded something they had for something they needed.

People traded to have people do things for them. They traded shells. They traded beads or stones. They even traded furs.

Another system was needed for trading. People used coins made of bronze. Coins had value. Everyone wanted coins. They could spend coins to get what they needed.

People called this money. They used gold (or silver or paper). It was worth an amount. They used money to buy something else.

One of the colonies issued the first paper money. People copied the money. They made fake money. Ben Franklin did not want this to happen. He printed notes with nature prints.

Congress passed a law that set the value of each coin. It based the value of coins on gold, silver, and copper. A mint made the first coins in 1793.

Later, the U.S. made paper money again. People called it "greenbacks." Can you guess its color?

Over time, the government added things to paper money. It had fine lines cut in it. And the government added a **seal** to paper money.

Every note also had an engraved signature. The government added color to paper money. Later, they added special thread. These things make it harder to copy money.

Today, people also use credit cards. They use ATM cards. They transfer money from the bank to pay bills. People do not carry as much cash.

Money

Directions: Darken the best answer choice.

1. What did a mint first make in 1793?
   - Ⓐ animals
   - Ⓑ coins
   - Ⓒ shells
   - Ⓓ fur

2. The **seal** on paper money is
   - Ⓐ the amount the bill is worth.
   - Ⓑ a way to close money in a bag.
   - Ⓒ an animal that lives in the ocean.
   - Ⓓ a design engraved to make it official.

3. What happened first in America?
   - Ⓐ People traded shells and beads.
   - Ⓑ People copied money.
   - Ⓒ The country made paper money.
   - Ⓓ A mint made coins.

4. Why has the government added thread to paper money?
   - Ⓐ Sometimes money goes through the washing machine.
   - Ⓑ It makes it harder to copy money.
   - Ⓒ People cannot tear money in half.
   - Ⓓ Thread is valuable.

5. Why did people call dollar bills "greenbacks"?
   - Ⓐ They had green lines on the back of the dollar.
   - Ⓑ They looked like turtles.
   - Ⓒ They were green.
   - Ⓓ They were made from leaves.

6. Picture a dollar bill. What do you *not* see on it?
   - Ⓐ a picture of a bank
   - Ⓑ numbers to tell how much it is worth
   - Ⓒ a Treasury seal
   - Ⓓ a signature

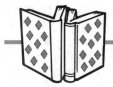
Fight for Freedom

One day, a woman rode a bus. Someone else got on. The first woman would not give up her seat. This renewed the Civil Rights movement. The woman was African American. Her name was Rosa Parks.

Rosa Parks kept her seat in 1955. She was tired from a long day of work. White people did not treat African Americans well. They looked down on them. Rosa did not like it.

People in the South were segregated. African Americans and whites had to stay apart. African Americans sat at the back of the bus. They did not go to the same schools.

Rosa Parks was born in Alabama. A secret group wanted to hurt African Americans. Rosa was afraid of them. She thought her house would be burned down.

Years later, a white person got on the bus. Rosa did not give up her seat. Police caught her. She went to trial.

Dr. Martin Luther King Jr. formed a group. His group told people not to ride the city buses. This **boycott** lasted for over a year.

The Supreme Court made a law. The law said not to separate people. African Americans and whites could ride buses. They could sit where they wanted.

Young people look to Rosa Parks as a role model. She stood up for what she believed.

Rosa Parks was brave. Her actions changed lives. She wanted African Americans and whites to get along. She said she was just "one of many who fought for freedom."

Fight for Freedom

One woman would not give up her seat on the bus. This renewed the Civil Rights movement. The woman was African American. Her name was Rosa Parks.

Rosa Parks kept her seat in 1955. She was weary from a long day of work. White people treated African Americans badly. Rosa did not like the way others looked down on people of her race.

People were segregated in the South. People of different races had to stay apart. African Americans had to sit at the back of the bus. They went to different schools.

Rosa Parks was born in Alabama. As a child, she feared a secret group who wanted to hurt African Americans. She was afraid her house would be burned down.

Years later, a white person wanted to sit on the bus. Rosa did not give up her seat. Police caught her. She went to trial.

Dr. Martin Luther King Jr. formed a group. His group told people not to ride the city buses. This **boycott** lasted for over a year.

Finally, the Supreme Court made a law. They said it was not legal to separate people on city buses and trains. People could sit wherever they wanted.

Rosa Parks served as a role model for young people. She stood up for what she believed was right.

Rosa Parks was brave. Her actions changed the lives of many people. She wanted African Americans and whites to get along. She said she was just "one of many who fought for freedom."

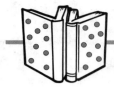

Fight for Freedom

One woman refused to give up her seat on the bus. A new chapter started in the Civil Rights movement. The woman was African American. Her name was Rosa Parks.

Rosa Parks kept her seat in 1955. She was weary from a long day of work. She was also tired of being mistreated. She did not like the way others looked down on people of her race.

People were segregated in the South. People of different races could not be together. African Americans had to sit at the back of the bus. They went to different schools.

Rosa Parks was born in Alabama. As a child, she feared a secret group who wanted to hurt minorities. She was afraid her house would be burned down.

Years later, Rosa did not give up her seat on the bus for a white person. Police arrested her. She went to trial.

Later, Dr. Martin Luther King Jr. formed a group. People from his group chose not to use the city bus line. This **boycott** lasted for over a year.

Finally, the Supreme Court made a law. They said it was not legal to separate people on city buses and trains.

Rosa Parks served as a role model for young people. She stood up for what she believed was right.

Her courage changed the lives of many people. She wanted people of different races to get along. She said she was just "one of many who fought for freedom."

Fight for Freedom

Directions: Darken the best answer choice.

1. Who would not give up a seat on the bus?
   - Ⓐ Dr. Martin Luther King Jr.
   - Ⓑ the Supreme Court
   - Ⓒ the NAACP
   - Ⓓ Rosa Parks

2. A **boycott** happens when people
   - Ⓐ say boys cannot ride the bus.
   - Ⓑ refuse to do something as a protest.
   - Ⓒ form a group.
   - Ⓓ sit where they want on a bus.

3. What happened next after Rosa Parks would not give up her seat?
   - Ⓐ Police arrested her.
   - Ⓑ People boycotted the city bus line.
   - Ⓒ She went to trial.
   - Ⓓ The Supreme Court made a law.

4. What is different today from when Rosa Parks grew up?
   - Ⓐ People ride buses.
   - Ⓑ African Americans and whites do not have to stay apart.
   - Ⓒ People do not treat others well.
   - Ⓓ African Americans live in the United States.

5. Why did Rosa Parks fight for civil rights?
   - Ⓐ She wanted people to be treated equally.
   - Ⓑ She wanted to be part of a group.
   - Ⓒ She wanted to follow Dr. Martin Luther King Jr.
   - Ⓓ She wanted to help young people.

6. Picture Rosa Parks on the bus. What do you see?
   - Ⓐ A white woman sitting down.
   - Ⓑ An African American woman carrying a dog.
   - Ⓒ An African American woman who was tired of being mistreated.
   - Ⓓ A white woman standing up.

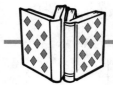

An Apple a Day

Who planted the first apple tree? No one knows for sure. People long ago ate apples. People in China grew apples. People ate dried apples in Egypt. Romans planted apple trees. Greeks liked to eat apples.

Greek doctors said apples were good for you. Roman doctors said the same thing. They told people to eat an apple after a meal. They thought apples helped people **digest** their food.

J. T. Stinson went to the World's Fair in 1904. He knew a lot about fruit. He said, "An apple a day keeps the doctor away."

The Swiss have a legend. A legend is an old story. The story is about William Tell. He used a bow and arrow. The king put his hat on a pole. He told people to bow down. Tell would not bow. The police caught him. They asked him to shoot an apple off his son's head. Then, he could go free. So he did.

A legend tells about Isaac Newton. He watched an apple fall. It fell in a straight line. Newton wanted to find out more. He learned about gravity. It is a force. It makes things fall.

People from Europe came to America. They brought apple seeds. They planted the seeds. People moved west. They kept planting apple seeds.

One story tells about Johnny Appleseed. His real name was John Chapman. John went to cider mills. A mill is a place that presses apples. They use the juice to make cider.

People gave John apple seeds. He dried the seeds. He put them in small bags. Then, John walked around the Midwest. He gave seeds to farmers. People say he walked barefoot. He wore a tin pot on his head.

People still eat apples today. You can take an apple for lunch. Apples make good snacks. Applesauce is good hot or cold. Enjoy an apple today!

An Apple a Day

Who planted the first apple tree? No one knows for sure. People long ago ate apples. The Chinese grew apples. People have found dried apples in Egypt. The Romans planted apple trees. Greeks liked to eat apples.

Greek doctors said apples were healthy. Roman doctors agreed. They told people to eat an apple after a meal. They thought apples helped people **digest** their food.

J. T. Stinson went to the World's Fair in 1904. Stinson knew a lot about fruit. He said, "An apple a day keeps the doctor away."

The Swiss have a legend. A legend is an old story. It is about William Tell. He was an archer. Tell would not bow down to the king's hat. The police caught him. They asked him to shoot an apple off his son's head. Then, he could go free. So he did.

A legend tells about Isaac Newton. He watched an apple fall. It fell in a straight line. Newton wanted to find out more. He learned about gravity. It is the force that makes things fall.

People from Europe came to America. They brought apple seeds. They planted the seeds. People moved west. They kept planting apple seeds.

One legend tells about Johnny Appleseed. His real name was John Chapman. John went to cider mills. They are places that press apples. They use the juice to make cider.

People at the mill gave John apple seeds. He dried the seeds. He put them in small bags. Then, John walked around the Midwest. He gave seeds to farmers. People say he walked barefoot. He wore a tin pot on his head.

People still eat apples today. You can take an apple for lunch. Apples make good snacks. Applesauce is good hot or cold. Enjoy an apple today!

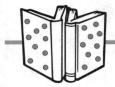

An Apple a Day

Who planted the first apple tree? No one knows for sure. People long ago ate apples. The ancient Chinese grew apples. Egyptians dried apples to eat. The Romans and Greeks planted apple trees and ate apples.

Greek doctors thought apples were healthy. Roman doctors said to eat an apple after a meal. They thought apples helped people **digest** their food.

In 1904, J. T. Stinson went to the World's Fair. The fair took place in St. Louis. Stinson knew a lot about fruit. He said, "An apple a day keeps the doctor away."

The Swiss have a legend about William Tell. He was an archer. The police arrested him because he would not bow down to the king. If he shot an apple off his son's head, he would be free. So he did.

Another legend tells about Sir Isaac Newton. He watched an apple fall to the ground. It fell in a straight line. He was curious and wanted to learn more. He studied gravity, the force that makes things fall.

Settlers from Europe traveled to America. They brought apple seeds with them. They planted the seeds. As settlers moved west, they planted more apple seeds.

A legend tells about Johnny Appleseed. His real name was John Chapman. He got apple seeds from cider mills. The mills pressed the apples and made cider from the juice.

Johnny dried the seeds and put them in small bags. Then, he walked around the Midwest. He gave the seeds to farmers. The legend says he walked barefoot. Some people say he wore an old tin pot for a hat.

Today, people eat apples in many ways. Apples make a great lunch food or snack. Applesauce is good to eat hot or cold. Enjoy an apple today!

An Apple a Day

Directions: Darken the best answer choice.

1. Who said, "An apple a day keeps the doctor away"?
   - Ⓐ Isaac Newton
   - Ⓑ William Tell
   - Ⓒ John Chapman
   - Ⓓ J. T. Stinson

2. When your body **digests** food,
   - Ⓐ your stomach breaks it down.
   - Ⓑ your body understands the food.
   - Ⓒ you breathe easier.
   - Ⓓ it turns your food into a snack.

3. What happened next after Johnny Appleseed went to the cider mill?
   - Ⓐ He dried the seeds.
   - Ⓑ He put the seeds in small bags.
   - Ⓒ He got some apple seeds.
   - Ⓓ He gave the seeds to farmers.

4. How is the legend of Isaac Newton different from the one about William Tell?
   - Ⓐ Newton watched a pear fall.
   - Ⓑ Newton wanted to learn about gravity.
   - Ⓒ Newton shot an apple off a tree.
   - Ⓓ Newton was caught by the police.

5. How is apple cider made?
   - Ⓐ The juice is pressed out of apples.
   - Ⓑ Apples are cooked in a pot.
   - Ⓒ The apples are dried in the sun.
   - Ⓓ Apples are dropped on the ground.

6. Picture Johnny Appleseed talking to someone. Who is it?
   - Ⓐ a doctor
   - Ⓑ a man with a bow and arrow
   - Ⓒ a farmer
   - Ⓓ a writer

Score the Goal!

Perhaps you played soccer today. You played with your friends. Another class formed the other team. You marked goals. You knew where to kick the ball. This is how people played soccer long ago. They did not always have rules. Games had large teams.

People have played soccer for many years. People in other places played early forms of soccer. They played soccer in China. They played in Central America. Greeks played a form of soccer. The Romans also played.

In Central America, players used a rubber ball. They played in a low place in the ground. They kicked the ball into baskets. The baskets were on the sidewalls. A ball went in the basket. It counted as a **goal**. A rubber ball is hard to kick. People from these countries still play soccer well.

In the Middle Ages, whole towns played the game. They did not care how many played on a team. People from the same town made up a team. They used landmarks for goals. They defended their goal. They made balls out of leather skins or pigskin. They stuffed the balls. The teams ran towards the ball. They all tried to kick it. They pushed each other. They wanted to get to the ball. These games got rough. People got hurt.

Ebenezer Cobb Morley formed a club. He talked to leaders from other clubs. They made rules for the game. Cobb called the game "football."

Some teams did not like the rules. They wanted to carry the ball. They tripped other people. The two groups split. One group played football (in America, this is called soccer). The other group played rugby.

The World Cup is a contest for soccer. It happens every four years. It is important. Some people think it is as great as the Olympics. Half the people on Earth play soccer. It is the most widely played game in the world.

Score the Goal!

Perhaps you played soccer at recess today. You played with your friends. Another class formed the other team. You marked goals. You knew where to kick the ball. This is how people played soccer long ago. Soccer games did not always have rules. Games had large teams.

People have played soccer for many years. People in other countries played early forms of the game. People played soccer in China. They played in Central and South America. The Greeks and Romans played a form of soccer.

In Central America, players used a rubber ball. They played in a large pit dug below the ground. They tried to kick the ball into baskets. The baskets were strapped along the sidewalls. A ball went into a basket. It counted as a **goal**. A rubber ball is hard to control. People from these countries play soccer well today.

During the Middle Ages, whole towns played the game. They did not care how many people played on a team. Each person on a team was from the same town. They used landmarks for goals and defended their goals. They made balls out of leather skins. Some balls were made of pigskin. The balls were stuffed with almost anything. The two teams ran towards the ball. They all tried to kick it. They pushed each other out of the way to get to the ball. These games got rough, and people got hurt.

Ebenezer Cobb Morley formed a club. He asked leaders from other clubs to meet. They made rules for the game. Morley called the game "football."

Some teams did not like the rules. They wanted to allow players to carry the ball. They tripped other players. The two groups split. One group played football (in America, this is called soccer). The other group played rugby.

The World Cup is a contest for soccer. It happens every four years. It is very important. Some people think it is as great as the Olympics. Half the people on Earth play soccer. This makes it the most widely played game in the world.

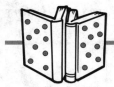

Score the Goal!

Perhaps you played soccer at recess or P.E. this week. Your friends and classmates formed a team. Kids from another class formed another team. You marked where to kick the ball to score a goal. Soccer played this way is much like soccer long ago. Many games of soccer did not have rules. Sometimes there were large teams.

People have played soccer for many years. Other countries had early forms of the game. People played soccer in China. They played in Central and South America. The Greeks and Romans played a form of soccer.

In Central America, players used a rubber ball. They played in a pit dug below ground level. They tried to kick the ball into baskets. The baskets were strapped along the sidewalls. If the ball went into a basket, it counted as a **goal**. A rubber ball is hard to control. People from these countries play soccer well today.

During the Middle Ages, whole villages would play the game. It didn't matter how many people were on a team. Each person on a team had to be from the same town. They used landmarks for goals and defended their goals. The balls were made out of leather skins. Some balls were made of pigskin. The balls were stuffed with almost anything. The masses of people ran towards the ball. They all tried to kick it. They pushed each other out of the way to get to the ball. These games got violent.

Ebenezer Cobb Morley formed a club. He asked leaders from other clubs to meet. They made official rules for the game. Morley called the game "football."

Some teams disagreed with the rules. They wanted players to carry the ball. They thought it was okay to trip other players. Finally, the two groups split. One group played football (in America, this is called soccer), and the other group played rugby.

The World Cup soccer tournament occurs every four years. Some people think it is as important as the Olympics. Almost half the people in the world play soccer. This makes it the most widely played game in the world.

Score the Goal!

Directions: Darken the best answer choice.

1. Where did players use a rubber ball?
   - Ⓐ China
   - Ⓑ Greece
   - Ⓒ Rome
   - Ⓓ Central America

2. A **goal** is
   - Ⓐ the other team.
   - Ⓑ when you score points.
   - Ⓒ the ball you kick.
   - Ⓓ the person who makes the rules.

3. What happened first?
   - Ⓐ People from the same town made a team.
   - Ⓑ People got a leather ball.
   - Ⓒ People ran towards the ball.
   - Ⓓ People got hurt.

4. How is soccer today like soccer long ago?
   - Ⓐ Players use a rubber ball.
   - Ⓑ Games have two teams.
   - Ⓒ We use a basket for a goal.
   - Ⓓ Players carry the ball.

5. The World Cup is a contest to see
   - Ⓐ which team has the most players.
   - Ⓑ which team brings the biggest cup.
   - Ⓒ which team plays the best.
   - Ⓓ which team has the best rules.

6. Where are the goals in soccer today?
   - Ⓐ in a hole in the field
   - Ⓑ in the middle of the field
   - Ⓒ on the sides of the field
   - Ⓓ at each end of the field

Dogs as Pets

People keep dogs as pets. Dogs also work.

Most dogs came from wolves. Wolves helped people hunt. Wolves looked after flocks. They kept animals together. They warned people. Wolves kept enemies away. People fed the wolves.

Wolves live together in packs. They are social animals. They can be good companions.

Long ago, wolves mated with wild dogs. People tamed wild dogs. Dogs helped people hunt for food. They watched people's homes. Dogs warned people about enemies.

Shepherds kept dogs. The dogs herded sheep. They guarded flocks. Dogs kept wild animals from getting the sheep.

People in China and Japan used dogs to hunt game. Dogs fought in wars. People gave dogs as gifts. They gave dogs to kings. Dogs had servants.

In Europe, people had lap dogs. Women kept them for comfort. People used dogs for many things. Dogs guarded houses. They turned **spits** over fires. Dogs hunted rats. People used dogs to hunt small game. Shepherds kept dogs. The dogs protected their flocks.

About 150 years ago, more people had pets. Families liked having pets. After World War II, people had more money. They spent money on pets.

People still like to have dogs for many reasons. Dogs make good friends. Some dogs look nice. Dogs can be interesting. They are fun to play with. Dogs are good pets.

Dogs as Pets

People have kept dogs as pets for many years. Often, dogs have served as working animals.

Most dogs came from wolves. People used wolves to hunt. Wolves looked after flocks. They kept animals together. They warned people about enemies. People made sure the wolves got food.

Wolves live together in packs. They are social animals. This makes them good companions.

Long ago, wolves mated with wild dogs. People tamed wild dogs. Dogs helped people hunt for food. People kept dogs to watch their homes. Dogs warned people about enemies.

Shepherds kept dogs to guard flocks. They used dogs to herd sheep. The dogs kept wild animals from getting the sheep.

In China and Japan, dogs hunted game. Some dogs fought in wars. People gave dogs as gifts. They gave dogs to kings. Kings gave dogs their own human servants.

In Europe, lap dogs became popular. Women kept them for comfort. Many people had dogs. They used their dogs for different things. Dogs guarded houses. They turned **spits** over open fireplaces. Dogs hunted rats. People used dogs to hunt small game. Shepherds used dogs to protect their flocks.

About 150 years ago, more people had pets. Families liked having dogs. After World War II, people had more money. They were willing to spend money on pets.

People still like to have dogs for many reasons. Dogs make good company. Some dogs are beautiful or interesting. Taking care of a pet gives people something to do. Many people think it is good to have a dog. Dogs will continue to be valuable pets.

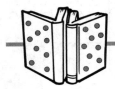

Dogs as Pets

Dogs have been popular as pets for many years. Often, dogs have served as working animals.

Dogs probably descended from wolves. People used wolves to hunt. Wolves could look after flocks and keep them together. They would warn people about enemies. People made sure the wolves got food.

Wolves live together in packs. They are social animals. This makes them good companions.

Long ago, wolves mated with wild dogs. People tamed wild dogs. People kept dogs to help hunt for food and watch their homes. Dogs could warn people about enemies.

People kept dogs to guard flocks of animals. Shepherds used dogs to herd sheep or cattle. The dogs kept wild animals from attacking the sheep.

In China and Japan, dogs were used as hunters and fighters. People gave dogs as gifts to kings and emperors. Kings gave dogs their own human servants.

In Europe, lap dogs became popular. Women kept them for comfort. Many people had dogs. They used their dogs for many things. Dogs guarded houses. They could turn **spits** over open fireplaces. Dogs hunted rats and other pests. People used dogs to hunt small game. Shepherds used dogs to protect their flocks against predators.

Having a pet became more common about 150 years ago. Families liked having pets. After World War II, people had more money. They were willing to spend money on pets.

People still like to have pet dogs for many reasons. Dogs make good company. Some dogs are beautiful or interesting. Taking care of a pet gives people something to do. Many people think the benefits of having a dog are greater than the costs. Dogs will continue to be valuable pets.

Dogs as Pets

Directions: Darken the best answer choice.

1. Where did people first have lap dogs?
   Ⓐ China
   Ⓑ Japan
   Ⓒ Europe
   Ⓓ Rome

2. In this story, **spit** means
   Ⓐ a long stick that holds meat.
   Ⓑ liquid from someone's mouth.
   Ⓒ a hole in the ground.
   Ⓓ an angry sound.

3. When were people willing to spend money on pets?
   Ⓐ when dogs guarded flocks
   Ⓑ before dogs fought in wars
   Ⓒ before World War II
   Ⓓ after World War II

4. A dog is most like a
   Ⓐ sheep.
   Ⓑ wolf.
   Ⓒ rat.
   Ⓓ cow.

5. Why do people like to keep dogs?
   Ⓐ Dogs help people.
   Ⓑ Dogs cost money.
   Ⓒ Dogs have tails.
   Ⓓ Dogs are ugly.

6. We call small dogs "lap dogs" because they
   Ⓐ pull sleds.
   Ⓑ drink water with their tongues.
   Ⓒ run around tracks.
   Ⓓ sit on laps when people sit down.

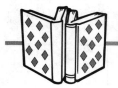

The Storyteller

Joseph Bruchac writes poems and stories. He tells these stories to other people. The stories are about his culture. Joe is part Native American. His tribe is Abenaki.

Joe went to college. He took wildlife classes. He wanted to save animals. He also took a writing class. He started reading poetry. He wanted to write poems. Now, Joe writes about the land. He writes about his past.

He tells old tales. The stories come from native people. They live in the Northeast. They live in the woods.

He tells stories to children. Schools ask him to come. He talks about native **culture**. Students listen to his stories.

"Stories build a sense of community. They draw people into new things," says Joe.

Native stories have lessons. They tell how to treat others. Joe cares about how people treat Earth. His stories teach. Joe wants to help kids. Stories show the right path in life.

Joe also writes songs. He sings in a group. His sister sings with him. His two sons sing in the group. The group is the Dawn Land Singers. They made a CD.

Native Americans are people. They are not pictures. They did not just live in the past. They live today. Joe helps native people. He keeps their culture alive. He tells stories.

The Storyteller

Joseph Bruchac writes poems and stories. He shares these stories with people. He tells stories about his Abenaki background.

Joe went to college. He took wildlife classes. He wanted to save animals. He also took a writing class. He started reading poetry. He decided to write poems. Now, Joe writes about the land. He writes about his past.

He tells traditional tales. The stories come from native people. They live in the northeastern woodlands.

He performs for children. Schools ask him to visit. He talks about native **culture**. Students listen to his stories.

"Stories build a sense of community. They draw people into new experiences," says Joe.

Native stories have lessons. They tell how to treat other people. Joe talks about how we should treat Earth. His stories teach. Joe wants to help kids. Stories show them the right path in life.

Joe also writes songs. He performs in a group. His sister and two sons sing with him. They call the group the Dawn Land Singers. They made a CD.

Native Americans are people. They are not pictures. They did not just live in the past. They live today. Joe helps native people. He keeps their culture alive. He tells stories.

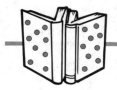

The Storyteller

Joseph Bruchac writes poetry and stories. He shares these stories with other people. He tells stories from his Abenaki background.

Joe went to college. He took classes in wildlife conservation. Then, he took a writing class. He started reading and writing poetry. Now, Joe writes about the land. He writes about his ancestry.

The storyteller tells tales about native people. These people live in the northeastern woodlands.

He performs for children. Schools ask him to visit. He discusses native **culture** with students. They listen to his stories.

"A story can build a feeling of community. It draws a person into a new experience," says Joe.

Native stories have lessons. They tell how people should treat each other. Joe talks about how people should act toward Earth. He wants his stories to bring knowledge. He wants to help kids. Stories can show them the right path in life.

Joe also writes songs. He performs in a group. His sister and two grown sons sing with him. The group is called The Dawn Land Singers. They recorded a CD.

Native Americans are people. They are not pictures. They did not just live in the past. They live in the present time. Joseph Bruchac helps native people keep their culture alive. He tells stories.

The Storyteller

Directions: Darken the best answer choice.

1. Joseph Bruchac's family comes from what group of Native Americans?
   - Ⓐ Dawn Land
   - Ⓑ Europe
   - Ⓒ Abenaki
   - Ⓓ Cherokee

2. Joseph Bruchac talks about native **culture**. He talks about their
   - Ⓐ customs and way of life.
   - Ⓑ yogurt.
   - Ⓒ concerts.
   - Ⓓ parents.

3. What did Joseph do before he started writing?
   - Ⓐ He read poetry.
   - Ⓑ He took wildlife classes.
   - Ⓒ He sang songs.
   - Ⓓ He talked to kids.

4. When children listen to his stories, they
   - Ⓐ look at a display.
   - Ⓑ write the words down.
   - Ⓒ see a movie.
   - Ⓓ learn something new.

5. How does Joseph Bruchac help native people?
   - Ⓐ He goes to Europe.
   - Ⓑ He is part Native American.
   - Ⓒ He lives in the foothills.
   - Ⓓ He tells stories.

6. What is one thing Joseph Bruchac does *not* do?
   - Ⓐ tell stories
   - Ⓑ draw cartoons
   - Ⓒ write poetry
   - Ⓓ sing songs

The World of Cartoons

A cartoon tells a story. It is like a book. People turn books into movies. Perhaps you have read a book that is now a movie.

Cartoons have animation. They have drawings. A film shows the sketches fast. It looks as if they move.

Artists place the pictures together. This takes many **frames**. The first cartoons used drawings done by hand.

Stop-motion uses objects. The artist takes a picture. Then, he or she moves the object. The artist takes another picture.

The artist puts the pictures on film. It looks as if the things move. A film shows twenty-four frames per second. The action looks smooth.

Some movies use puppets. The *Star Wars* films do this. Yoda was a puppet.

Children enjoy cartoons. Even grown-ups watch them. The first cartoons were short. People went to the movies. A funny cartoon played first. Then, people saw the main film.

Walt Disney made a short cartoon. It was *Little Red Riding Hood*. Disney made a rabbit. Then, he made a mouse. It became Mickey Mouse.

He made a film about Mickey Mouse. Later, he made a film called *Steamboat Willie*. It had sound. It was seven minutes long.

One cartoon showed Tom and Jerry. Tom was a cat. Jerry was a mouse. People still watch them today.

Computers make things seem real. Pictures come to life. *The Lion King* had 3-D pictures. It also had drawings done by hand.

Each cartoon takes a lot of time, work, and creativity.

The World of Cartoons

A cartoon tells a story like a book. People turn books into movies. Perhaps you have read a book that is now a movie.

Cartoons have animation. They use drawings. A film shows the sketches fast. It looks as if they move.

Artists put the pictures together. This takes many **frames**. The first cartoons used drawings done by hand.

Stop-motion uses objects. The artist takes a picture. He or she moves the object a tiny bit. Then, the artist takes another picture.

The artist puts the pictures together on film. It looks as if the objects move. A film shows twenty-four frames per second. The action looks smooth.

Some stop-motion uses puppets. The *Star Wars* films have these scenes. Yoda was a puppet.

Children like cartoons. Even grown-ups watch them. The first cartoons were short. People went to the movies. A funny cartoon played first. Then, they saw the main film.

Walt Disney made a short cartoon. It was *Little Red Riding Hood*. Disney created a rabbit. Then, he made a mouse. It became Mickey Mouse.

Later, he made a film called *Steamboat Willie*. It had sound. It was seven minutes long.

There were cartoons about Tom and Jerry. Tom was a cat, and Jerry was a mouse. People still watch them today.

Computers make things seem alive. A program makes still pictures come to life. *The Lion King* had 3-D pictures. It also had drawings done by hand.

Each cartoon takes a lot of time, work, and creativity.

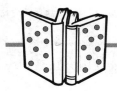
The World of Cartoons

A cartoon tells a story like a book. People turn some books into movies. Perhaps your favorite book is also a movie.

Cartoons use animation. They have drawings. A film shows the drawings fast. It looks as if the drawings move.

Artists put the pictures together. This takes many **frames**. The first cartoons used drawings done by hand.

Stop-motion uses objects. The person making the film takes a picture. He or she moves the object a tiny bit. Then, he or she takes another picture.

The artist puts the pictures together on film. It looks as if the still objects move. A movie shows twenty-four frames per second. This makes the movement look smooth.

Some stop-motion uses puppets. The *Star Wars* films have stop-motion scenes. Yoda was a puppet.

Children enjoy cartoons. Even grown-ups watch cartoons. Years ago when people went to the movies, they saw a cartoon "short." It played before the main film.

Walt Disney made a short cartoon. It was *Little Red Riding Hood*. Disney's first animal character was a rabbit.

Then, he created a mouse. It became Mickey Mouse. Disney made a film about Mickey Mouse. He later made a cartoon called *Steamboat Willie*. It had sound. It was seven minutes long.

One cartoon showed Tom and Jerry. Tom was a cat, and Jerry was a mouse. People still watch them today.

Computers make things seem alive. A program makes still pictures come to life. *The Lion King* had 3-D computer pictures. It had computer images and drawings done by hand.

Each cartoon takes a lot of time, effort, and creativity.

The World of Cartoons

Directions: Darken the best answer choice.

1. Who made Mickey Mouse?
   - Ⓐ Tom and Jerry
   - Ⓑ Walt Disney
   - Ⓒ Willie
   - Ⓓ Yoda

2. In animated movies, a **frame** is
   - Ⓐ something you hang on a wall.
   - Ⓑ what you build a house around.
   - Ⓒ a small picture that is part of a strip of film.
   - Ⓓ the way the cartoon character stands.

3. What does a stop-motion artist do after he or she takes a picture of an object?
   - Ⓐ The artist moves the object a little bit.
   - Ⓑ The artist makes a drawing.
   - Ⓒ The artist takes another picture.
   - Ⓓ The artist watches a cartoon.

4. How is *The Lion King* different from *Steamboat Willie*?
   - Ⓐ *The Lion King* was about a mouse.
   - Ⓑ *The Lion King* used computers.
   - Ⓒ *The Lion King* was a cartoon.
   - Ⓓ *The Lion King* used puppets.

5. How does it appear as if animated objects move?
   - Ⓐ They have strings.
   - Ⓑ The artists film only at night.
   - Ⓒ Many still pictures are put together and shown fast.
   - Ⓓ Artists use magnets to move objects.

6. What do you see when you watch a cartoon?
   - Ⓐ a computer screen
   - Ⓑ live actors on a stage
   - Ⓒ pictures of your friends
   - Ⓓ drawings

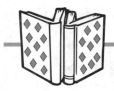

LEARN TO DRAW

Drawing is fun. You can draw what you see and make it look the way you want it to look.

The first step is to decide what to draw. Then, look for the basic shapes in the object. Does it have circles? Look to see which way lines go. Some lines are straight. Some are curved. Some have angles.

You can start by drawing the center of the picture, such as a flower. You can also draw the main part of the object. When you draw a house, start with the basic shape. Then, add the details.

Another way to learn to draw is to use a grid. A grid has rows and columns of squares. It has letters and numbers. Place the grid over a photograph. Find the first square. Look at what is in that square. Draw the same thing in the first square on your paper. Keep drawing pieces of the picture until you finish the whole picture. This is a good way to practice drawing.

Remember, there is no wrong way to draw. What matters is that you like what you draw. It is okay to look at something and draw that object. Everyone sees things in different ways. What you draw will not look the same as what your friend draws.

Practice drawing. Do not look at the paper. Look at the object you are trying to draw. Follow the **contour** of the object with your eyes. Tell your hand to draw the same shape. Remember not to look at your hand.

It is hard to draw people. You can use basic shapes. Use an oval for the head. Draw circles and tubes for body parts. Look for lines that show how a person moves.

Experiment with drawing. Just use a pencil. Add color in different ways. You will be amazed at what you can learn to draw.

LEARN TO DRAW

Drawing is fun. You can draw what you observe and make it look the way you want it to look.

The first step is to decide what to draw. Then, look for the basic shapes in the object. Does it have circles? Look to see the direction of the lines. Some lines are straight, and some are curved. Some lines have angles.

You can start by drawing the center of the picture, as in the center of a flower. You can also draw the main part of the object. When you draw a house, start with the basic shape. Then, add the details.

Another way to learn to draw is to use a grid. A grid has rows and columns of squares. The rows and columns have letters and numbers. Place the grid over a photograph. Find the first square. Look at what is in that square. Draw the same thing in the first square on your paper. Keep drawing pieces of the picture until you finish the whole picture. This is a good way to practice drawing.

Remember, there is no wrong way to draw. The important thing is that you like what you draw. It is okay to look at something and draw that object. Everyone sees things with a different perspective. What you draw will not look the same as what your friend draws.

Practice drawing without looking at your paper. Look at the object you are trying to draw. Follow its **contour** with your eyes. Tell your hand to draw the same shape. Remember not to look at your hand.

It is hard to draw people. You can use basic shapes. Use an oval for the head. Draw circles and tubes for body parts. Look for lines that follow a person's actions.

Experiment with drawing. Draw with a pencil or pen in black and white. Add color in different ways. You will be amazed at what you can learn to draw.

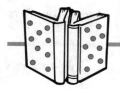

Learn to Draw

Drawing is enjoyable. You can sketch what you observe and make it look the way you want it to look.

The first step is to decide what to draw. Then, look for the basic shapes in the object. Does it have circles? Look to see the direction of the lines. Some lines are straight, and some are curved. Lines with angles come to a point.

You can begin by drawing the center of the picture, as in the center of a flower. Sketch the main part of the object. When you design a house, start with the basic shape, and then add details.

Another way to practice is to use a grid. A grid has rows and columns of squares. The rows and columns have letters and numbers. Place the grid over a photograph. Find the first square, and look at what is in that square. Draw the same thing in the first square on your paper. Keep drawing pieces of the picture until you complete the whole picture.

Remember, there is no wrong way to draw. Your picture portrays what you observe. The important thing is that you like what you draw. It is okay to look at something and draw that object. Everyone sees things with a different perspective. What you draw will not look exactly like the picture your friend draws.

Practice drawing without looking at your paper. Look at the item you are trying to draw. Follow its **contour** with your eyes, and move your hand at the same time. While remembering not to look at your hand, tell it to draw the same shape.

It is difficult to draw people. Use an oval for the head, and then draw basic shapes like circles and tubes for body parts. Look for lines that follow a person's movements.

Experiment with drawing. Draw with a pencil or pen in black and white. Add color in various ways. Try using different textures. You will be amazed at what you can learn to draw.

Learn to Draw

Directions: Darken the best answer choice.

1. Where do you place a grid?
   - Ⓐ over a photograph
   - Ⓑ on a model
   - Ⓒ on the table
   - Ⓓ on your computer

2. The **contour** of an object is
   - Ⓐ its color.
   - Ⓑ its outline.
   - Ⓒ its hand.
   - Ⓓ its actions.

3. What do you do after you decide what to draw?
   - Ⓐ draw the center of the picture
   - Ⓑ look for basic shapes
   - Ⓒ add details
   - Ⓓ color your picture

4. A person's head is like
   - Ⓐ a square.
   - Ⓑ a circle.
   - Ⓒ an oval.
   - Ⓓ a triangle.

5. Why is it okay to draw the same thing as someone else?
   - Ⓐ You like the object.
   - Ⓑ Everyone sees things in different ways.
   - Ⓒ You will not like your drawing.
   - Ⓓ You are using the computer.

6. Pretend you are drawing a house. What details can you add?
   - Ⓐ eyes
   - Ⓑ leaves
   - Ⓒ windows
   - Ⓓ wheels

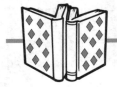

To Buy or Not to Buy

Have you ever wanted what your friend had? Perhaps you watched a TV show. You saw a commercial for a new toy. You wanted to buy the toy.

Advertising tries to sell things. Companies want you to buy things. They want you to spend money.

People buy things other people have. They want to try something new. New products cost more at first. People will pay the price. Later, the price drops.

Some products sell well. Then, they come out in a new form. People think that they need the new model. The company sells more this way.

Music in ads creates a mood. A product might have a **jingle**. This helps you remember it. When you go to the store, you remember to buy it.

Companies make toys based on movies. Kids want to buy the toys. Characters from cartoons are used on products.

Top 5 Buys for Kids

✓ Cell phone

✓ MP3 player

✓ Video game system

✓ Bike

✓ Art supplies and books

Schools have TV programs. Students watch educational shows. They also see ads. You might see an ad on your school bus. A book cover might have an ad. Bulletin boards have ads.

The Internet has many ads. Watch out! Some online ads ask for personal information. There are games for you to play online. The games try to sell a product. Web sites mix ads with content. Learn to tell what is an ad and what is not.

When you shop for food, read the labels. See what is in the food you buy. You will know what you are eating. You can tell if it is good for you.

Advertising can tell you about a product. But it can also fool you. Beware of what you buy.

Best Deals This Week | Contact Us | Biggest Scams in History

To Buy or Not to Buy

Have you ever wanted something that your friend had? Perhaps you watched a TV show. You saw a commercial for a new toy. You wanted to buy the toy.

Advertising tries to sell things. The company wants you to buy their products. They want you to spend money.

People buy things their friends have. They are excited to try something new. New products often cost more at first. People will pay the price. Later, the price drops.

Some products sell very well. Later, they come out in new versions. People think that they need the new model. The company sells more things this way.

Music in ads creates a mood. A product might have a song or a **jingle**. This helps you remember the product. When you go to the store, you will remember to buy it.

Top 5 Buys for Kids

✓ Cell phone

✓ MP3 player

✓ Video game system

✓ Bike

✓ Art supplies and books

Companies make toys based on cartoons and movies. Kids want to buy the toys. Favorite characters from cartoons are used on products.

Schools have TV programming. Students watch educational shows. They also see ads. You might see an ad on your school bus. Book covers and bulletin boards have ads.

The Internet has many ads. Watch out! Online ads may ask for personal information. Companies create activities for you to do online. The games try to sell their product. Web sites combine ads with the content. Learn the difference between ads and information.

When you shop for food, read the labels. See what is in the food you buy. You will know what you are eating and if it is good for you.

Advertising can tell you more about a product. But it can also fool you. Beware of what you buy.

Best Deals This Week | Contact Us | Biggest Scams in History

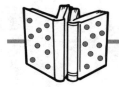

To Buy or Not to Buy

Have you ever wanted something that your friend had? Perhaps you watched your favorite TV show and saw a commercial for a new toy. You wanted to buy the toy.

Advertising tries to sell things. The company wants you to buy their products. They want you to spend money.

People buy popular things. They are excited to try something new. New products often cost more at first. People will pay the price. Later, the price drops when the item isn't as popular.

Some products sell very well. Later, they come out in new versions. People think that they need the new model. The company sells more things this way.

Music in ads creates a mood or a style. A product might have a song or a **jingle**. This helps you remember the product. When you go to the store, you will remember to buy the item.

Top 5 Buys for Kids

✓ Cell phone

✓ MP3 player

✓ Video game system

✓ Bike

✓ Art supplies and books

Companies make toys related to cartoons and movies. Kids want to buy the toys. Favorite characters from cartoons are used on products. Shoes, backpacks, and other things have characters from movies on them.

Schools have TV programming. Students watch educational shows. They also see advertising. You might see an ad on your school bus. Book covers and bulletin boards have ads.

The Internet has many advertisements. Watch out! Online ads may ask for personal information. Companies create activities for you to do online. The games try to sell their product. Web sites combine ads with the content. Learn to tell the difference between ads and information.

When you shop for food, read the labels. See what is in the food you buy. You will know what you are eating and if it is healthy.

Advertising can tell you more about a product, but it can also fool you. Beware of what you buy.

Best Deals This Week | Contact Us | Biggest Scams in History

To Buy or Not to Buy

Directions: Darken the best answer choice.

1. What do we call advertising on TV?
   - Ⓐ a show
   - Ⓑ a Web site
   - Ⓒ a billboard
   - Ⓓ a commercial

2. A **jingle** is a
   - Ⓐ short song that advertises a product.
   - Ⓑ bell you ring when you buy something.
   - Ⓒ doorbell at a store.
   - Ⓓ new model of a product.

3. What happens second?
   - Ⓐ You see a commercial for a new toy.
   - Ⓑ The toy is no longer new and popular.
   - Ⓒ You ask your parents to buy the toy.
   - Ⓓ The price of the toy drops.

4. Which two things are most similar?
   - Ⓐ TV commercials and advertisements at movies
   - Ⓑ posters and jingles
   - Ⓒ online games and outdoor games
   - Ⓓ backpacks and school buses

5. Why should people read labels on food?
   - Ⓐ to find out if they need a fork or a spoon
   - Ⓑ to find out if their friends eat it
   - Ⓒ to find out what is in the food
   - Ⓓ to find out if it has a toy

6. Think about an advertisement. What does it try to do?
   - Ⓐ teach you to sing
   - Ⓑ get you to buy a product
   - Ⓒ help you to read better
   - Ⓓ show you a cartoon

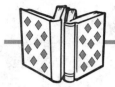
The Many Uses of Pumpkins

Pumpkins are the world's biggest fruit. They are related to squash. Pumpkins came from Central America. They grow almost everywhere. They do not grow at the South Pole.

The Native Americans used pumpkin. They cut it into long strips. They built a fire. Then, they **roasted** and dried the strips. They wove mats using the strips. Native Americans ate the seeds. They also used the seeds for medicine.

Other people use pumpkin for cures. They use it for snakebites. People in China say it takes away pain.

Colonists ate pumpkin. They cut off the top. They took out the seeds. They put in milk and spices. They added honey. The pumpkin baked in hot ashes.

Now, we make pumpkin pie. We make soup and bread. People use it in cookies. They make muffins. People feed pumpkin to animals. Elephants in zoos eat it.

In other countries, people eat pumpkin. People eat it as a vegetable. Some people roast it with beef.

People in Switzerland eat pumpkin. They make many foods. They roll small balls of pumpkin and flour. They cook them in hot water. They also use the seeds to make salad oil. They eat pumpkin with chocolate, too.

Most of the fruit is safe to eat. People cook the fruit's meat. They roast the seeds. The seeds make a good snack. It is safe to eat the flowers. People make salad with the leaves.

Pumpkins grow on vines. Some grow on bushes. People harvest them. Pumpkins can be stored. Keep them in a warm, dry place. They keep best with the stem on.

Try something new! Find a way to eat the world's largest fruit.

The Many Uses of Pumpkins

Giant pumpkins are the world's biggest fruit. They belong to the squash family. Pumpkins came from Central America. They grow almost everywhere. They do not grow in Antarctica.

The Native Americans used pumpkins for many things. They cut strips of pumpkin. Then, they built a fire and **roasted** long strips over it. They dried the strips and wove mats from them. Native Americans ate the seeds. They used the seeds for medicine.

Other people use pumpkin for medicine. People use it for snakebites. People in China use pumpkin to take away pain.

Colonists ate pumpkin. They cut off the top. Then, they scooped out the seeds. They put in milk and spices. They added honey. They baked the pumpkin in hot ashes.

Now, we make pumpkin pie. We also make soup and bread. Pumpkin can be used in cookies and muffins. People feed pumpkin to animals. Elephants in zoos eat pumpkin.

In other countries, people eat pumpkin. People eat it as a vegetable. Some people roast pumpkin with beef.

People in Switzerland use pumpkin for many foods. They make small balls of pumpkin and flour. They cook them in boiling water. They also make salad oil with the seeds. They eat pumpkin with chocolate, too.

Most of a pumpkin is safe to eat. People cook the fruit's meat. They roast the seeds. The seeds make a good snack. It is safe to eat the flowers. People make salad with the leaves.

Pumpkins grow on vines. Some grow on bushes. People harvest them. Pumpkins can be stored. Keep them in a warm, dry place. They keep best with the stem still on.

Try something new! Find a way to eat the world's largest fruit.

Magazine Article

The Many Uses of Pumpkins

It may surprise you to learn that pumpkin is a fruit. In fact, giant pumpkins are the world's largest fruit. They are members of the squash family. Pumpkins first came from Central America. Now, they grow on every continent except Antarctica.

The Native Americans used pumpkins for many things. They cut long strips of pumpkin and **roasted** them over an open fire. Then, they dried the strips and wove them into mats. Native Americans used the seeds for food and medicine.

Other people use pumpkin for medicine. Some people think it will get rid of freckles. People from China use it as a cure for snakebites. They believe pumpkin takes away pain.

Colonists ate pumpkin. They cut off the top. Then, they scooped out the seeds. They put in milk, spices, and honey. They baked the pumpkin in hot ashes.

Now, we make pumpkin pie. People feed pumpkin to animals. Elephants in zoos eat pumpkin. People use pumpkin to make soup, pie, bread, cookies, and other things.

In other countries, people eat pumpkin in different ways. Often, people eat pumpkin as a vegetable. Some people roast pumpkin with beef. Pumpkin can be eaten with chocolate, too.

People in Switzerland use pumpkin for many foods. They cook small balls of pumpkin and flour in boiling water. They also make salad oil with pumpkin seeds.

Almost all of a pumpkin is safe to eat. People cook the meat of the pumpkin. They roast the seeds. Pumpkin seeds make a good snack. It is safe to eat the flowers. Some people make salad with the leaves.

Pumpkins grow on vines or bushes. People harvest them. Pumpkins can be stored. Keep them in a warm, dry place. They keep best with the stem still on.

Try something new! Find a way to eat some of the world's largest fruit.

The Many Uses of Pumpkins

Directions: Darken the best answer choice.

1. Who wove mats with pumpkin?
   - Ⓐ the Chinese
   - Ⓑ the Native Americans
   - Ⓒ the colonists
   - Ⓓ the zookeepers

2. People **roast** pumpkin. In this article that means
   - Ⓐ put it in hot water.
   - Ⓑ use it in a salad.
   - Ⓒ cook it in a hot oven or over a fire.
   - Ⓓ put it in a can.

3. What did the colonists do last?
   - Ⓐ They baked pumpkin in hot ashes.
   - Ⓑ They cut off the top.
   - Ⓒ They put in milk and spices.
   - Ⓓ They took out the seeds.

4. Pumpkins keep best
   - Ⓐ with the stem cut off.
   - Ⓑ with the flowers cut off.
   - Ⓒ with the vine cut off.
   - Ⓓ with the stem still on.

5. What part of a pumpkin do people *not* eat?
   - Ⓐ the seeds
   - Ⓑ the rind
   - Ⓒ the leaves
   - Ⓓ the meat

6. Picture a pumpkin. Where is it?
   - Ⓐ in the refrigerator
   - Ⓑ on a tree
   - Ⓒ in a pumpkin patch
   - Ⓓ in a hole

Answer Sheet

Name: _____

Title: _____

Page: _____

1. Ⓐ   Ⓑ   Ⓒ   Ⓓ
2. Ⓐ   Ⓑ   Ⓒ   Ⓓ
3. Ⓐ   Ⓑ   Ⓒ   Ⓓ
4. Ⓐ   Ⓑ   Ⓒ   Ⓓ
5. Ⓐ   Ⓑ   Ⓒ   Ⓓ
6. Ⓐ   Ⓑ   Ⓒ   Ⓓ

Answer Sheet

Name: _____

Title: _____

Page: _____

1. Ⓐ   Ⓑ   Ⓒ   Ⓓ
2. Ⓐ   Ⓑ   Ⓒ   Ⓓ
3. Ⓐ   Ⓑ   Ⓒ   Ⓓ
4. Ⓐ   Ⓑ   Ⓒ   Ⓓ
5. Ⓐ   Ⓑ   Ⓒ   Ⓓ
6. Ⓐ   Ⓑ   Ⓒ   Ⓓ

Answer Sheet

Name: _____

Title: _____

Page: _____

1. Ⓐ   Ⓑ   Ⓒ   Ⓓ
2. Ⓐ   Ⓑ   Ⓒ   Ⓓ
3. Ⓐ   Ⓑ   Ⓒ   Ⓓ
4. Ⓐ   Ⓑ   Ⓒ   Ⓓ
5. Ⓐ   Ⓑ   Ⓒ   Ⓓ
6. Ⓐ   Ⓑ   Ⓒ   Ⓓ

Answer Sheet

Name: _____

Title: _____

Page: _____

1. Ⓐ   Ⓑ   Ⓒ   Ⓓ
2. Ⓐ   Ⓑ   Ⓒ   Ⓓ
3. Ⓐ   Ⓑ   Ⓒ   Ⓓ
4. Ⓐ   Ⓑ   Ⓒ   Ⓓ
5. Ⓐ   Ⓑ   Ⓒ   Ⓓ
6. Ⓐ   Ⓑ   Ⓒ   Ⓓ

Answer Sheet

Name: _____

page 17
1. Ⓐ Ⓑ Ⓒ Ⓓ
2. Ⓐ Ⓑ Ⓒ Ⓓ
3. Ⓐ Ⓑ Ⓒ Ⓓ
4. Ⓐ Ⓑ Ⓒ Ⓓ
5. Ⓐ Ⓑ Ⓒ Ⓓ
6. Ⓐ Ⓑ Ⓒ Ⓓ

page 37
1. Ⓐ Ⓑ Ⓒ Ⓓ
2. Ⓐ Ⓑ Ⓒ Ⓓ
3. Ⓐ Ⓑ Ⓒ Ⓓ
4. Ⓐ Ⓑ Ⓒ Ⓓ
5. Ⓐ Ⓑ Ⓒ Ⓓ
6. Ⓐ Ⓑ Ⓒ Ⓓ

page 57
1. Ⓐ Ⓑ Ⓒ Ⓓ
2. Ⓐ Ⓑ Ⓒ Ⓓ
3. Ⓐ Ⓑ Ⓒ Ⓓ
4. Ⓐ Ⓑ Ⓒ Ⓓ
5. Ⓐ Ⓑ Ⓒ Ⓓ
6. Ⓐ Ⓑ Ⓒ Ⓓ

page 77
1. Ⓐ Ⓑ Ⓒ Ⓓ
2. Ⓐ Ⓑ Ⓒ Ⓓ
3. Ⓐ Ⓑ Ⓒ Ⓓ
4. Ⓐ Ⓑ Ⓒ Ⓓ
5. Ⓐ Ⓑ Ⓒ Ⓓ
6. Ⓐ Ⓑ Ⓒ Ⓓ

page 21
1. Ⓐ Ⓑ Ⓒ Ⓓ
2. Ⓐ Ⓑ Ⓒ Ⓓ
3. Ⓐ Ⓑ Ⓒ Ⓓ
4. Ⓐ Ⓑ Ⓒ Ⓓ
5. Ⓐ Ⓑ Ⓒ Ⓓ
6. Ⓐ Ⓑ Ⓒ Ⓓ

page 41
1. Ⓐ Ⓑ Ⓒ Ⓓ
2. Ⓐ Ⓑ Ⓒ Ⓓ
3. Ⓐ Ⓑ Ⓒ Ⓓ
4. Ⓐ Ⓑ Ⓒ Ⓓ
5. Ⓐ Ⓑ Ⓒ Ⓓ
6. Ⓐ Ⓑ Ⓒ Ⓓ

page 61
1. Ⓐ Ⓑ Ⓒ Ⓓ
2. Ⓐ Ⓑ Ⓒ Ⓓ
3. Ⓐ Ⓑ Ⓒ Ⓓ
4. Ⓐ Ⓑ Ⓒ Ⓓ
5. Ⓐ Ⓑ Ⓒ Ⓓ
6. Ⓐ Ⓑ Ⓒ Ⓓ

page 81
1. Ⓐ Ⓑ Ⓒ Ⓓ
2. Ⓐ Ⓑ Ⓒ Ⓓ
3. Ⓐ Ⓑ Ⓒ Ⓓ
4. Ⓐ Ⓑ Ⓒ Ⓓ
5. Ⓐ Ⓑ Ⓒ Ⓓ
6. Ⓐ Ⓑ Ⓒ Ⓓ

page 25
1. Ⓐ Ⓑ Ⓒ Ⓓ
2. Ⓐ Ⓑ Ⓒ Ⓓ
3. Ⓐ Ⓑ Ⓒ Ⓓ
4. Ⓐ Ⓑ Ⓒ Ⓓ
5. Ⓐ Ⓑ Ⓒ Ⓓ
6. Ⓐ Ⓑ Ⓒ Ⓓ

page 45
1. Ⓐ Ⓑ Ⓒ Ⓓ
2. Ⓐ Ⓑ Ⓒ Ⓓ
3. Ⓐ Ⓑ Ⓒ Ⓓ
4. Ⓐ Ⓑ Ⓒ Ⓓ
5. Ⓐ Ⓑ Ⓒ Ⓓ
6. Ⓐ Ⓑ Ⓒ Ⓓ

page 65
1. Ⓐ Ⓑ Ⓒ Ⓓ
2. Ⓐ Ⓑ Ⓒ Ⓓ
3. Ⓐ Ⓑ Ⓒ Ⓓ
4. Ⓐ Ⓑ Ⓒ Ⓓ
5. Ⓐ Ⓑ Ⓒ Ⓓ
6. Ⓐ Ⓑ Ⓒ Ⓓ

page 85
1. Ⓐ Ⓑ Ⓒ Ⓓ
2. Ⓐ Ⓑ Ⓒ Ⓓ
3. Ⓐ Ⓑ Ⓒ Ⓓ
4. Ⓐ Ⓑ Ⓒ Ⓓ
5. Ⓐ Ⓑ Ⓒ Ⓓ
6. Ⓐ Ⓑ Ⓒ Ⓓ

page 29
1. Ⓐ Ⓑ Ⓒ Ⓓ
2. Ⓐ Ⓑ Ⓒ Ⓓ
3. Ⓐ Ⓑ Ⓒ Ⓓ
4. Ⓐ Ⓑ Ⓒ Ⓓ
5. Ⓐ Ⓑ Ⓒ Ⓓ
6. Ⓐ Ⓑ Ⓒ Ⓓ

page 49
1. Ⓐ Ⓑ Ⓒ Ⓓ
2. Ⓐ Ⓑ Ⓒ Ⓓ
3. Ⓐ Ⓑ Ⓒ Ⓓ
4. Ⓐ Ⓑ Ⓒ Ⓓ
5. Ⓐ Ⓑ Ⓒ Ⓓ
6. Ⓐ Ⓑ Ⓒ Ⓓ

page 69
1. Ⓐ Ⓑ Ⓒ Ⓓ
2. Ⓐ Ⓑ Ⓒ Ⓓ
3. Ⓐ Ⓑ Ⓒ Ⓓ
4. Ⓐ Ⓑ Ⓒ Ⓓ
5. Ⓐ Ⓑ Ⓒ Ⓓ
6. Ⓐ Ⓑ Ⓒ Ⓓ

page 89
1. Ⓐ Ⓑ Ⓒ Ⓓ
2. Ⓐ Ⓑ Ⓒ Ⓓ
3. Ⓐ Ⓑ Ⓒ Ⓓ
4. Ⓐ Ⓑ Ⓒ Ⓓ
5. Ⓐ Ⓑ Ⓒ Ⓓ
6. Ⓐ Ⓑ Ⓒ Ⓓ

page 33
1. Ⓐ Ⓑ Ⓒ Ⓓ
2. Ⓐ Ⓑ Ⓒ Ⓓ
3. Ⓐ Ⓑ Ⓒ Ⓓ
4. Ⓐ Ⓑ Ⓒ Ⓓ
5. Ⓐ Ⓑ Ⓒ Ⓓ
6. Ⓐ Ⓑ Ⓒ Ⓓ

page 53
1. Ⓐ Ⓑ Ⓒ Ⓓ
2. Ⓐ Ⓑ Ⓒ Ⓓ
3. Ⓐ Ⓑ Ⓒ Ⓓ
4. Ⓐ Ⓑ Ⓒ Ⓓ
5. Ⓐ Ⓑ Ⓒ Ⓓ
6. Ⓐ Ⓑ Ⓒ Ⓓ

page 73
1. Ⓐ Ⓑ Ⓒ Ⓓ
2. Ⓐ Ⓑ Ⓒ Ⓓ
3. Ⓐ Ⓑ Ⓒ Ⓓ
4. Ⓐ Ⓑ Ⓒ Ⓓ
5. Ⓐ Ⓑ Ⓒ Ⓓ
6. Ⓐ Ⓑ Ⓒ Ⓓ

page 93
1. Ⓐ Ⓑ Ⓒ Ⓓ
2. Ⓐ Ⓑ Ⓒ Ⓓ
3. Ⓐ Ⓑ Ⓒ Ⓓ
4. Ⓐ Ⓑ Ⓒ Ⓓ
5. Ⓐ Ⓑ Ⓒ Ⓓ
6. Ⓐ Ⓑ Ⓒ Ⓓ

Answer Key

page 17
1. D
2. B
3. C
4. B
5. A
6. B

page 21
1. B
2. C
3. A
4. C
5. D
6. A

page 25
1. B
2. A
3. A
4. C
5. C
6. D

page 29
1. B
2. B
3. D
4. A
5. C
6. A

page 33
1. A
2. C
3. B
4. C
5. A
6. D

page 37
1. C
2. A
3. B
4. D
5. B
6. A

page 41
1. B
2. A
3. C
4. C
5. D
6. B

page 45
1. A
2. C
3. D
4. B
5. B
6. A

page 49
1. C
2. B
3. A
4. A
5. C
6. B

page 53
1. B
2. A
3. D
4. B
5. C
6. B

page 57
1. B
2. D
3. A
4. B
5. C
6. A

page 61
1. D
2. B
3. A
4. B
5. A
6. C

page 65
1. D
2. A
3. C
4. B
5. A
6. C

page 69
1. D
2. B
3. A
4. B
5. C
6. D

page 73
1. C
2. A
3. D
4. B
5. A
6. D

page 77
1. C
2. A
3. B
4. D
5. D
6. B

page 81
1. B
2. C
3. A
4. B
5. C
6. D

page 85
1. A
2. B
3. B
4. C
5. B
6. C

page 89
1. D
2. A
3. C
4. A
5. C
6. B

page 93
1. B
2. C
3. A
4. D
5. B
6. C